The Little Book of
RUGBY
LEGENDS

PAUL**MORGAN** and ALEX**MEAD**

The Little Book of
RUGBY
LEGENDS

This edition first published in the UK in 2006
By Green Umbrella

© Green Umbrella Publishing 2007

www.greenumbrella.co.uk

Publishers Jules Gammond and Vanessa Gardner

Printed and bound in China

ISBN 1-905009-53-4

CONTENTS

CONTENTS

PHIL
BENNETT

Name: Philip Bennett
Born: 24 October 1948
Country: Wales
Position: Fly-half
Debut: 22 March 1969 v France
Caps: 29
Points: 16

Two Lions tours stand head and shoulders above the rest: the vintage of 1971 and 1974, when they won in New Zealand and South Africa respectively. The 1974 Lions won a titanic Test series, 3-0 with the final match drawn, and they achieved that historic triumph against the Springboks with a magician at outside-half, Llanelli's Phil Bennett.

The man with the stunning sidestep and an almost unerring right boot left an indelible mark on rugby union.

Against the Boks, he formed a dream partnership with Gareth Edwards at half-back, and he was to score more than 100 points on the tour. His 50-yard try in the second Test in Pretoria, which the Lions won 28-9, will live with all who saw it, Bennett finishing it off with a final sidestep that left full-back Ian McCallum utterly bamboozled. Many regarded this as the game of Bennett's life. And on his return to Britain, rugby league came calling, St Helens offering him £40,000 over a three-year period – a vast sum in those days.

The man known throughout the rugby world as Benny turned them down, just as he had refused an offer from Halifax when Bennett was still playing youth rugby for his village team as a 17-year-old.

Within weeks of his triumphant homecoming from South Africa, Bennett's life turned upside down as he and his wife Pat lost their first child, Stewart, because of a heart defect.

For a time rugby meant nothing to Bennett, but he slowly came to terms with the tragedy, and by 1977 he agreed to tour again with the Lions – this time as captain. He thus became only the second Welshman, after John Dawes, to lead a genuine Lions squad.

That trip to New Zealand proved an exacting one for the tourists as they lost the series 3-1, although Bennett still managed to score 100 points on the tour.

His famous sidestep has become celebrated across the world and in 1973 he was the chief architect of the game's most famous try, scored by the Barbarians against New Zealand at Cardiff Arms Park.

Simply referred to today as 'that try', Bennett started a legendary length-of-the-field move with some mesmerizing sidesteps near his own try-line to turn defence into attack, and several passes later the move was completed when Edwards dived over in the corner.

There was huge pressure on Bennett right from the start of his international career as he was asked to take over the famed Wales No 10 jersey from The King, Barry John.

"That was a tough act to follow but the Llanelli wizard rose to the challenge," remembered Ireland international Phil Matthews in The Sunday Times. "His 50-metre try in the second Test at Pretoria saw him swerve and sidestep through the Springbok defence in a way I could only dream of repeating."

But take over from John he did, with all the panache expected of a Welsh fly-half, winning 29 caps for Wales, eight of them as captain.

Bennett made his Test debut in 1969 during an 8-8 draw with France, becoming the first Welsh replacement to be capped.

With John in the side, some of his early Test rugby was spent at full-back, but after inheriting the No 10 jersey he prospered and by the time Bennett retired from international rugby in 1978, he held the Welsh scoring record, with 166 points.

Bennett's glory days weren't restricted to the Lions. He won three Grand Slams and four Triple Crowns with Wales, while he enjoyed 16 wonderful seasons with Llanelli, the Scarlets winning four successive Welsh Cup finals from 1973-76.

He also helped manufacture the most famous victory in Llanelli's history, as they beat the All Blacks 9-3 in 1972.

Delme Thomas, the Llanelli captain that day, remembered a piece of Bennett magic when he recently spoke to the Western Mail. As Bennett received the ball to make a clearance to touch, he found himself staring into the combative eyes of Grant Batty, the quick and uncompromising All Black winger who had come on as a replacement for Bryan Williams.

Bennett, with one of those magical sidesteps, glided past Batty before kicking to touch.

"I'll never forget the look on Batty's face as he clutched at empty air," Thomas said. "It was the moment I knew we had won."

Bill McLaren, the famous rugby commentator, summed up what so many thought about Bennett. "His adhesive hands, his educated boot, his nose for space and those shimmering sidesteps... could light up a game with pure genius," said McLaren.

Bennett ended his international career on an emotional high, captaining the Wales team of 1978 to a Grand Slam. In the final game, the great man scored two tries in a 16-7 victory over France at Cardiff. "The crowd won the game for us that day," he said. "Yes, the boys played with huge spirit but that emotional singing from the crowd made it. Once they started, there was no way France were ever going to score.

"I'd decided before the game that I would retire. I'd had a couple of good seasons, the crowd were very nice to me and I thought, 'Why spoil it by hanging on?'" Bennett was just 29 when he took his curtain call.

With Bennett and several other Wales stars retiring at that time, it took the Principality 27 years to win another Grand Slam.

Bennett was a man full of humility and he was delighted by his recent induction into the International Rugby Hall of Fame.

"To be inducted alongside the likes of Gareth Edwards, Gerald Davies and Mervyn Davies is such an honour," said Bennett. "It makes me feel very humble when I think back to my days playing for Felinfoel Youth, Llanelli Schoolboys, my beloved Scarlets and Wales."

Bennett moved into broadcasting after his playing days were over and he now commentates on the game for television.

ABOVE
Bennett kicks to touch during the British Lions tour match against South Africa, 1974.

MIDDLE
Bennett, Lions Captain, leads out his team to play Waikato on July 16, 1977 in Hamilton, New Zealand.

FAR LEFT
Bennett in action during the Test Series between New Zealand and the British Lions in July 1977.

SERGE
BLANCO

Name: Serge Blanco
Born: 31 August 1958
Country: France
Position: Full-back
Debut: 8 November 1980 v South Africa
Caps: 93
Points: 233

In every era comes a player who sums up the soul of a rugby team. In the 1980s that role belonged to Serge Blanco, the mercurial French international who defined everything good about his side in that decade. Born in 1958 in Venezuela, Blanco had no peer in the No 15 jersey at that time and only a handful in the history of rugby.

He won a staggering 93 caps for France, after his family moved to the country when he was a child. Blanco's versatility was evident by the fact that he won 12 of those caps on the wing, while he is regarded as the iconic full-back, winning a place in Rugby World's Team of the Century. He had pace to spare and at 6ft 1in and approaching 14st he had the power to make him one of the most elusive full-backs to play the game. His ability to change speed also made him a nightmare for opponents.

Luckily for Blanco, the World Cup kicked off while he was in his pomp and although New Zealand won the first tournament in 1987, for many the fondest memory is Blanco's try in the semi-final against Australia, when he battled injury to send his side through.

In front of just 18,000 spectators at Sydney's Concord Oval and with the game locked at 24-24, Blanco struck. Receiving the ball 30 metres out, he flew towards the corner on an angled run, scoring with a full-length dive to beat Tommy Lawton. Didier Camberabero's touchline conversion gave France a 30-24 victory.

John Reason, writing in The Daily Telegraph, said: "I never thought I would see a game to rival the one played between the Barbarians and the All Blacks in Cardiff in 1973, but this one did.

"The French came back from 9-0, 15-12 and 24-21 down and then at the death a surging move involving Champ, Lagisquet, Berbizier, Mesnel, Charvet, Berbezier again and Lagisquet again saw Rodriguez in support and Blanco forgetting his injured hamstring and going for his life and a try in the corner to put France in the final."

That try was typical of Blanco – who captained France 17 times – and the French of that era. Flair emanated from all parts of the team and the plaudits were quick to follow. France not only reached that first World Cup final but won Grand Slams in 1981 and 1987, as well as taking at least a share of the Five Nations Championship a further four times in the Eighties.

Blanco made his Test debut against South Africa in Cape Town in 1980 and although the French lost 37-15, it was the start of an 11-year career that brought him a France record of 38 tries, a tally that remained unbeaten by any full-back as the 2006 Six Nations drew to a close.

Blanco's elegant running style, creativity and inventive spirit epitomised the flamboyance for which French rugby is admired. He was an 'old school' player, smoking 60 cigarettes a day throughout his career (he gave up a year after retiring from the game), and still turning in performances that shook the rugby world.

David Campese is a player in the same mould as Blanco and the great Aussie often lamented the change of attitude that arrived with professionalism. "The emphasis is on winning, not entertaining," Campese said. "The creative aspect has gone and so have the characters, people like Serge Blanco, who always seemed to play with a smile on his face. Now it's a job. They're all told what to say and what not to say."

No one could have told a free spirit like Blanco what to do. Attacking from his own line and creating a try out of nothing were commonplace to him, no matter how big the occasion. In 1991, England and France met at Twickenham in a Grand Slam decider. Just 12 minutes into the game, Blanco lit the blue touchpaper for one of the greatest tries ever seen when he fielded a missed penalty attempt and launched a 100-yard counter-attack, which ended with Philippe Saint-Andre scoring under the posts.

His philosophy on the game is simple. "There are too many outside interests ruling the game and the financial rewards for the television companies and federations apply great pressure on teams to win," Blanco said. "The only way to make rugby a spectacle again is to make sure players are encouraged to express themselves."

Rugby was cruel to Blanco at the end, his final Test bringing defeat as France lost to England in the 1991 World Cup quarter-final in Paris.

But at least he bowed out in England in style, making a dazzling, try-scoring appearance in December 1991 as the Barbarians beat Leicester 29-21 in the annual Christmas holiday fixture.

LEFT
Blanco was a hugely athletic full-back.

FAR LEFT
Honours flowed in Blanco's magnificent career.

Steve Bale, writing in The Independent, summed up his impact: "People talk about Blanco's supposed shortage of speed but his capacity for opening up defences with power and acceleration, mesmerising changes of pace and direction, and the most delicate passing subtlety seemed completely unimpaired yesterday. As he will not play in England again, it was a privilege to watch the last farewell. Keeping such a man under control is asking the impossible."

Blanco's final club game ended in similar fashion, his beloved Biarritz losing the 1992 national championship final to Toulon.

But there was no way Blanco was going to leave the sport forever. He became president of Biarritz Olympique, seeing them become French champions in 2002.

He was also made president of France's national professional league, the Ligue Nationale de Rugby, ensuring his status as one of the most powerful men in the game.

Life outside rugby has seen him open the Serge Blanco Hotel and Thalassotherapy Centre in Hendaye in 1991 (other hotels have followed), and in 1992 The Serge Blanco range, with its striking 15 logo, was launched, leading to the opening of 50 shops.

DAVID
CAMPESE

Name: David Ian Campese
Born: 21 October 1962
Country: Australia
Position: Wing
Debut: 14 August 1982 v New Zealand
Caps: 101
Points: 315

David Campese played his last Test for the Wallabies in December 1996, and so prolific was he that his world record of 64 tries was still unsurpassed, and in fact not even threatened by anyone in the top 10 nations, a decade later. The winger started life on the international stage in 1982 – long before the Super 14 – at his club Randwick. And he went on to win a sensational 101 caps for Australia, lifting the 1991 World Cup along the way.

But it wasn't just his try-scoring (and the occasional drop-goal) that ensured Campese, who is of Italian descent, stood out from the crowd. It was his style and his approach to the game, from his trademark goose-step to the way he would attack from places where others wouldn't dare – even from behind his own posts.

His finest hour came in that 1991 World Cup in Europe. He failed to score in the final as Australia beat England 12-6 at Twickenham, but he had already illuminated the tournament with a brilliant display in the semi-final against New Zealand at Lansdowne Road.

"Campese brought the sparkle back to rugby in the twinkling of a few star-studded strides," wrote John Mason of The Daily Telegraph, commenting on that 16-6 semi-final victory. "In routing the peddlers of caution, the purveyors of the unimaginative and second-rate, the extraordinary Campese also brought down New Zealand, the world champions."

His try was sumptuous, the right-wing popping up on the left to take a pass from Nick Farr-Jones, break the All Blacks line and arrow to the corner.

But the second was even better. Campo (as he is known throughout the world of rugby) made it with a nonchalant flip pass over his shoulder, centre Tim Horan accepting the gift to scurry over and leave the Kiwis too big a mountain to climb. It was a sublime moment from a rugby genius.

Although he didn't score in the final, Campese had a significant hand in the victory. His comments in the run-up to the game were credited with forcing England to change their style. Will Carling's team had rumbled through to the final with a forward-dominated game plan, but Campese teased them in the days prior to the big match, helping to create the pressure that prompted a sudden change in England's philosophy. England's attempts to use their backs more in the final backfired and, despite a clear supremacy up front, the men in white were to finish as losers.

Campese's own philosophy throughout his career was simple. "I don't know what I'm going to do next, so how can anyone else?" he once said, high-lighting in a nutshell the problems opponents had trying to curb his wondrous talents.

He ended the 1991 World Cup with six of Australia's 17 tries and was voted Player of the Tournament.

Campese grew up outside Canberra before moving to Sydney, making his international debut aged 19 against New Zealand at Christchurch in 1982. He kicked off with a try, too, as Australia lost 23-16.

He scored again against the All Blacks two weeks later, in an historic 19-16 win for the Wallabies in Wellington, ensuring he was well and truly on the rugby world map.

That chance came after Campese showed outstanding form in the ACT and Australia Under-21 sides, and his break came when a number of Wallabies withdrew from that 1982 trip to New Zealand. He never looked back.

In the UK he left an indelible mark long before that World Cup as he was part of a new breed of Australia player: one of a group that helped win a Grand Slam (tour victories over England, Scotland, Ireland and Wales) for the Wallabies in 1984.

Campese was aided and abetted by a group of world-class Wallabies on that 1984 tour, including Michael Lynagh, Mark Ella and Nick Farr-Jones. Those four victories, which started with a 19-3 win at Twickenham against England, ensured the Wallabies' place in the new world order.

His duals with New Zealand were the stuff of legend, and in 1986 he helped Australia to their first Bledisloe Cup triumph in New Zealand for 37 years.

But it wasn't all glory for Campo because, like many geniuses, he had his flaws. His most famous blunder cost Australia the 1989 series against the Lions. In the third Test, he tried to initiate a counter-attack

LEFT
Campese was a
huge fan of Sevens,
here in action
against Scotland
in 1993.

FAR LEFT
The world's most
prolific try-scorer,
Campese powers
through against Italy.

from behind his own try-line, was struck by a moment of indecision and threw a risky pass to full-back Greg Martin. The ball went to ground and Ieuan Evans pounced to win the Test – and the series – for the Lions.

Campese was pilloried by some for the error, but most rugby fans saw sense, realising that one or two flaws in his make-up was a small price to pay for such outrageous ability. Lions and England centre Jeremy Guscott said: "Campese tries things, and that is part of his genius. Remove the risk and he would be half the player."

Campese became the first Australian to play 100 Tests when the Wallabies took on Italy in 1996 and a few weeks later he played his final Test, at Cardiff Arms Park against Wales. He failed to score but the Wallabies ensured a winning send-off for Campo, with a 28-19 victory.

A great advocate of sevens, Campese helped Australia to a Hong Kong Sevens title in 1983 and went on to coach the national sevens team to the bronze medal in the 1998 Commonwealth Games in Malaysia.

After holding a number of other coaching roles, in 2006 he was appointed as a consultant for South Africa's Sharks in the Super 14.

In January 2002, he was awarded the Order of Australia Medal for his services to rugby, and he still owns a sports shop, near Sydney Harbour.

DANIE
CRAVEN

Name: Daniel Hartman Craven
Born: 11 October 1910
Country: South Africa
Position: Scrum-half
Debut: 5 December 1931 v Wales
Caps: 16
Points: 6

With museums, awards and stadiums named after him, the influence of Daniel (Danie) Hartman Craven on South African rugby was evidently immense. It's rare to find an individual who excelled not only as a player but also as a coach and then a rugby administrator. And from his first cap in 1931 up until his death in 1993, Craven remained one of the pivotal figures at the forefront of South African rugby during its most turbulent times.

Although his playing career spanned just 16 caps – it was curtailed by the onset of World War Two – Craven managed to fit plenty into them.

He made his debut against Wales in 1931 at scrum-half as part of Bennie Osler's team that toured the British Isles. Having overcome Wales 8-3 in Swansea, the side beat Ireland by the same scoreline and then Scotland 6-3, with Craven grabbing his first international try.

It was a taste of things to come for Craven, as winning was something he was to prove adept at both as a player and a coach.

His rugby life was no doubt enhanced by the fact he studied at the famous Stellenbosch University – where the stadium and museum are named after him – and it was during his time there that he earned his first caps.

After the successful tour of the British Isles, Craven went on to play in seven Tests against the Wallabies – winning five of them, including two in Australia on the 1937 tour. It was on that same tour that Craven first captained the Springboks – against the All Blacks in Wellington – and although he was on the wrong side of a 13-7 scoreline, the tide soon turned. With Craven directing operations, the Springboks fought back to beat New Zealand 13-6 and 17-6 to secure an impressive 2-1 Test-series victory.

To add a further element of history-making, Craven appeared at fly-half and No 8 as well as in his usual role of scrum-half – a feat that, together with an earlier appearance in the centre, meant he represented South Africa in an unprecedented four positions in Test rugby. To add to his astonishing versatility, he also had a bash at full-back for a touring match against Queensland.

Craven certainly made the most of his international appearances. As if beating Australia and New Zealand on their own turf wasn't enough, which itself followed an unbeaten three-Test tour of Britain and Ireland, he also managed to fit in the visit of the British & Irish Lions in 1938.

Having assumed the captaincy, Craven led his side to a 2-1 Test-series victory, winning the first two matches 26-12 and 19-3 before succumbing in the third Test – a dead rubber – by 21-16.

The Second World War was then to put a stop to his playing career, but Craven had already achieved a fantastic amount and was widely regarded as the finest scrum-half of his generation. His achievements on the playing field were many, but his off-field involvement would outweigh all of them.

Coaching at his beloved Stellenbosch University from 1947 to 1991, Craven also put his rugby nous to good use for the national side, working as a selector and coach from 1949 until 1956. During his time of influence, the Springboks whitewashed the All Blacks 4-0 and won ten matches in a row. On the 1951-52 tour of Britain, Craven's side not only completed a Grand Slam but also won fans far and wide for their powerful brand of rugby. At Murrayfield the Boks triumphed 44-0 against Scotland – an incredible margin in those times of the three-point try. His influence from the touchline was so great that he's still talked about as one of the finest rugby coaches in Springbok history.

Even after all of this, Craven's devotion and passion for rugby remained as strong as ever and, to satisfy his appetite for the game, he became president of the SA Rugby Board in 1956 and from 1957 represented South Africa on the International Rugby Board – becoming chairman when it was his nation's turn.

His tenure as president was to last 37 years until the day he died and it was a period in which South Africa suffered its most controversial and difficult times as apartheid caused the rest of the world to look upon the country with disdain and eventually boycott them.

Even before their exile, it was a struggle to find games and it was the work of Craven that ensured they did play, fixtures in the Eighties against South America, New Zealand Cavaliers and a World XV giving South Africa's top players a taste of top-class rugby.

The influence of rugby in South African politics was so great that the sometimes-controversial Craven once said: "We can change South Africa on the rugby field." In meeting with the exiled African National Congress, he attempted to do just that.

His lifetime's work came to a fitting conclusion with the unity of the South African Football Union in 1992, a year before he died.

On top of all of his rugby work, Craven managed to gain three doctorates (four if you include the honorary one) in social anthropology, psychology and physical education, he worked as a teacher, soldier and professor, and he found time to pen several books on different aspects of the game, from coaching to history. He was also awarded honorary citizenship of Lindley, his birthplace in the Orange Free State, and Stellenbosch.

Even outside of South Africa, Craven had many admirers, not least Argentina – a side with whom the Springboks now contest the Danie Craven Trophy. At the inaugural contest for the trophy in 2004, the chief executive of Argentina Rugby, Christian Ramos, said of Craven: "Our rugby would not be where it is today if South Africa had not helped us get off the ground in the 1960s. Danie Craven was a great friend to us."

LEFT
Craven was a leader, known across South Africa as Mr Rugby.

FAR LEFT
Craven was president of the South African union for an incredible 37 years.

GERALD
DAVIES

Name: Thomas Gerald Reames Davies
Born: 7 February 1945
Country: Wales
Position: Wing
Debut: 3 December 1966 v Australia
Caps: 46
Points: 72

The epitome of attacking, running rugby, Welsh legend Gerald Davies has gained an army of admirers. Lions captain Willie John McBride likened watching Davies in full flight to "art in motion" and fellow Welsh international Cliff Morgan said of the man: "He wasn't the biggest of men, but he could sidestep, slink past or outspring almost anyone."

And his qualities weren't overlooked by those in the stands either, with commentator Bill McLaren one of his biggest fans. In his book Dream Lions, he wrote: "Davies was a gifted entertainer and often the spark plug to deeds of derring-do by his colleagues in the Cardiff and London Welsh clubs, and on the international scene. Even though he was small in stature, he tackled like the crack of doom and quickly embraced the modern concept of wingers acting as auxiliary full-backs. Frequently, too, he worked in liaison with his Welsh and Lions team-mate JPR Williams to create dazzling switch moves out of defence which left opposing defenders on the wrong foot."

A student of Queen Elizabeth Grammar School in Camarthen, Davies first came into the public eye when helping Loughborough Colleges take the Middlesex Sevens title in 1966. Moving to Cardiff for a teaching job later that year, Davies gained his first call-up for Wales – against the touring Wallabies. Playing in the centre, Davies suffered defeat, as was the case in his next three Internationals. The sequence was broken against England, when Davies ran in a brace of tries – his first on the international stage – in a 34-21 victory. Impressive as the feat was, centre Keith Jarrett overshadowed it with 19 points on his debut.

Nonetheless, after seven caps, Davies had done enough to gain selection for the British & Irish Lions tour to South Africa. Despite having a back injury, Davies still managed nine matches on the tour, including the third Test. Not only did he wow the locals with a 50-yard try against Boland but he was considered by many to be the most creative Lions back in the one Test he played.

The best, though, was still to come for Davies. Back with Wales, the side was beginning to offer glimpses of their true potential as they stormed to three wins in the 1969 Five Nations but were held 8-8 by France and denied the Grand Slam.

A trip to New Zealand followed and, after defeat in the first Test, it was on the internal flight that tour manager Clive Rowlands asked Davies to take up a berth on the wing. At the time Davies regarded such a move as effectively a demotion, but it was a switch that would ultimately lead to him becoming one of the greatest players of all time.

Wales suffered a second defeat to the All Blacks, but the tourists didn't go home empty-handed as Davies scored his third try for Wales in the 19-16 win over Australia in Sydney.

By this time Davies was a student at Cambridge University – where he earned Blues in 1968, 1969 and 1970 – and his studies meant he rested from international duty in 1970.

The break obviously did him good, as 1971 was the most successful in his career. First, Wales took their first Grand Slam since 1952, doing so in breathtaking style and with Davies playing a key role throughout. Their romp to the title almost came undone in only the second game. Scotland had looked to have snatched victory at Murrayfield, before Davies turned on the magic to dash past the bedazzled defenders and touch down in the corner. A kick from John Taylor – dubbed the "greatest conversion since St Paul" – brought Wales a dramatic victory and nothing was now going to stop the Welsh all-stars from clinching the Grand Slam.

The side had timed their run of form to perfection as no sooner had the Five Nations been brought to a close than a Lions side packed with Welshmen (London Welsh alone provided seven) was heading to New Zealand. A narrow 9-3 first-Test win for the tourists was followed by a heavy defeat – although Davies did manage two tries – before the speedster was on hand again with a third Lions Test try to help John Dawes's men into a 2-1 series lead that proved unassailable for the All Blacks.

Davies played in ten of the 26 matches in New Zealand and scored ten tries, including four in one match against Hawke's Bay. He came back to the UK as a legend. As McLaren wrote: "He returned with his reputation heightened and continued to impress as a wonderfully gifted wing with an elegance and style that was distinctive – pattering steps, the light-footed surge of pace and always with a thought for his colleagues."

Davies was unavailable to tour with the Lions in 1974 (to South Africa) and 1977 (New Zealand), but his achievements on the 1971 expedition were enough to confirm his status as a world great.

Wales' success in the 1970s undoubtedly softened the blow for missing those Lions tours as they played the kind of rugby that is still talked of in reverential tones across the world. To that initial Grand Slam in 1971 they added two further Slams in 1976 and 1978 – the last coming in Davies's final year as an international player.

For his swansong, Davies toured Australia with Wales and captained the side in his 46th and final appearance. It ended in a 19-17 defeat, but Davies scored one more try to take his tally to 20 – level with Gareth Edwards – and make him Wales' joint top try-scorer until Ieuan Evans arrived on the scene some years later.

Davies became a journalist with The Times after his retirement and was awarded a CBE in 2002. He was selected be on the WRU panel that selected the successor to coach Mike Ruddock, in April 2006.

ABOVE
Davies scores against Ireland at Cardiff Arms Park.

FAR LEFT
A Lions legend, Davies was a key member of the 1974 side that won in New Zealand.

JONATHAN
DAVIES

Name: Jonathan Davies
Born: 24 October 1962
Country: Wales
Position: Fly-half
Debut: 20 April 1985 v England
Caps: 32
Points: 81

It's hard enough to establish yourself as a legend in one sport, let alone two. But that is what Welshman Jonathan Davies managed to achieve, becoming a star of both rugby union and rugby league. A mercurial outside-half in the mould of predecessors such as Cliff Morgan, Barry John and Phil Bennett, Davies had the ability to dazzle and captivate fans from all over the world, and from both rugby codes.

Born in Trimsaran, Davies made a spectacular entrance to Test rugby, marking his Wales debut against England in 1985 with a try and drop-goal in a 24-15 victory.

Along with his prowess with ball in hand, he became something of a drop-goal expert, kicking 13 in Test matches, a record that still stood in 2006.

One of his finest days in union came in the first World Cup in 1987, where Davies guided Wales to third place, still their best-ever finish in the competition. That tournament also saw Davies captain Wales for the first of four occasions, in a pool match against Canada.

Davies, who was made captain of Neath before being transferred to Llanelli, played in six World Cup matches that season, but he saved his best to last, inspiring his side to a 22-21 victory over Australia in the third-place play-off.

That World Cup finish set the ground work for a Triple Crown victory in 1988, Wales' only defeat that season coming against the French, 10-9. Against Scotland, Davies scored one of the finest tries seen at Cardiff Arms Park when, receiving Robert Jones's reverse pass under pressure, he prodded a delicate grubber kick in front of the Scottish back row and beat Derek White to the touchdown.

Little did Davies know it at the time but that Triple Crown was to be his final success in a Wales jersey. After two thumping defeats by New Zealand on Wales' 1988 summer tour, and a humiliating loss to Romania the following December, Davies made the decision to 'go north' and signed a £225,000 deal with rugby league side Widnes.

A procession of union players had moved to league, but few can have made the same impact as Davies, who set records at every turn, playing for Great Britain and starring for Wales in the 1995 Rugby League World Cup.

At Widnes, Davies won virtually every domestic medal in the game and in 1991 he shattered the club's points record for a season with 342. The same year, he was voted First Division Player of the Year by his fellow professionals. Davies was also the fastest player in rugby league history to score 1,000 points.

One of his greatest days in the 13-man code came in a Great Britain shirt when he scored a spectacular try to beat the 1994 Australians at Wembley. It was vintage Davies: first, a dummy to beat the Australia cover, then a searing 50-yard dash to the line that lives long in the memory.

Peter Higham, chairman of Warrington, for whom Davies played for two years, summed up his effect in league: "He's one of the best players ever to have come north – possibly the best. It's a pity he's 33 and not 23. He's a one-off and is going to be difficult to replace."

Warrington coach Brian Johnson added: "The last thing you would want to do is to stifle his creative ideas. Jonathan is one of the unique few who can be considered great players and when you have talent that is well above the norm, it is not always easy to conform to set patterns of play.

"It's not as if he runs around doing crazy things. Sometimes he does things that are contrary to the accepted way of playing, but it is never ridiculous. And when you examine his success rate at creating openings out of nothing, you are not inclined to discourage him."

When rugby union became professional in 1995, it was inevitable that many of those players who had gone to league would return. Davies was the first.

By that time he was 33 and could only be expected to play a cameo role. Although he played five more times for Wales in 1996 and 1997, he was never going to repeat his former glories. He was at least able to go out on a high of sorts; his final match, against England in 1997, saw him share the stage with Will Carling and Rob Andrew, who also played their last Test match that day.

Davies was a maverick throughout his career, and explained his philosophy on the game in The Independent, saying: "What depresses me about many different games these days is the number of players who always take the safety-first option. I don't know if it is the fault of coaches or rigid team plans, but we don't seem to have many players prepared to take a chance and allow their natural ability to come through. That's what spectators want to see: players trying something different.

"The more unexpected, the more exciting it can be. All right, so you get a slagging-off if it goes wrong but it's still worth doing. Anything you do when the opposition are least expecting it throws them into confusion and when they are confused they are vulnerable."

After his playing career ended, Davies, who was awarded an MBE in 1995, established himself as one of the foremost commentators on the game, working for the BBC as an analyser of both league and union.

ABOVE
Davies came back to Cardiff, after union turned professional, in 1995.

MIDDLE
Davies was a star in Rugby league, here scoring for Great Britain, against Australia, in 1994.

FAR LEFT
Davies holds the Regal Trophy aloft in 1992.

LAWRENCE
DALLAGLIO

Name: Lawrence Bruno Nero Dallaglio
Born: 10 August 1972
Country: England
Position: No 8/Blindside flanker
Debut: 18 November 1995 v South Africa
Caps: 77
Points: 80

When Wales fly-half Iestyn Harris was asked to assess the strengths and weaknesses of England's team during the 2003 World Cup, he discovered that much of the good work that team put in revolved around one player – Lawrence Dallaglio. Stop Dallaglio and you stop England was what Harris concluded in 2003, by studying tapes of their matches. The No 8 was the platform for so much of England's best play in the tournament, and so it turned out in the final itself.

Trailing to a try from Lote Tuqiri, it was Dallaglio who set England off on the move that led to Jason Robinson's try and his side's recovery, which ended with a match-winning drop-goal from Jonny Wilkinson. Remarkably, when the final whistle blew in Sydney, Dallaglio had played in every minute of England's 2003 World Cup campaign.

Dallaglio is a natural leader and one of the first things Clive Woodward did when he took over as England coach in 1997 was to make the Wasps player his captain, even though he only had 15 caps to his name.

Dallaglio had a tough start to his reign with an autumn series that saw England take on New Zealand (twice), Australia and South Africa in a four-week spell. England emerged with two draws, one each against Australia and New Zealand.

One of the reasons Dallaglio was handed the captaincy was his leading role on the Lions' 2-1 series victory over South Africa the previous summer. Unfortunately, his captaincy lasted just 14 Tests as he resigned in 1999 following accusations about his private life in a British tabloid newspaper.

His resignation came soon after one of his worst days in an England shirt, the 32-31 defeat by Wales at Wembley. That cost Dallaglio a Grand Slam, and the captaincy passed to Martin Johnson.

Dallaglio, however, always received the full backing of Woodward and when Johnson retired after the World Cup triumph in 2003, it was Dallaglio who took the helm once again.

His run in the England team coincided with the formation of the most prolific back row in history. Dallaglio combined with Neil Back and Richard Hill, and together they won more caps as a unit than any back row before them.

One of Dallaglio's main rivals for the captain's armband in 2004 was Gloucester's Phil Vickery, who was eager to acknowledge his credentials.

LAWRENCE**DALLAGLIO**

"Anyone who can stand up and say Lawrence isn't a good choice is being a bit of an idiot," Vickery said. "I know that if I was going to war then he would be someone I'd want with me in the trenches."

Johnson was in agreement, adding: "Lawrence is a born leader. If you had a group of blokes stuck in the jungle, he would become a leader of that group. He is a strong, charismatic character who enjoys taking responsibility and thrives on it."

Rob Howley, who played alongside Dallaglio for Wasps and the Lions, is another who recognised the wisdom of appointing Dallaglio in the wake of the 2003 World Cup. "Replacing Johnson was never going to be easy but in picking Lawrence, Clive has taken the pressure off the situation," he said. "If anyone else had been given the job they would have found themselves and their record being readily compared to that of Johnson."

A one-club man, Dallaglio signed for Wasps as a teenager and made his debut in September 1993. He was to become an indispensable figurehead of the club, helping Wasps to a succession of domestic and European honours, including the 2006 Powergen Cup.

He was made club captain when Rob Andrew left for Newcastle in 1995 and years later his experience and leadership proved critical on a number of high-profile occasions. In 2004 Wasps lifted the Heineken Cup after beating French giants Toulouse in the final at Twickenham, and a year later Wasps were back at the stadium to clinch their third successive English title.

The Little Book of **RUGBY** LEGENDS

He won every honour the game has to offer, but his first came in 1993, when he was part of the England team that surprised many by winning the Sevens World Cup. That trophy helped him win his first full England call-up, for the tour to South Africa in 1994.

Dallaglio, who is of Italian descent, went on three Lions tours but in his case it was the best that came first, as he launched himself on the world stage with a series of superb performances as the Lions beat South Africa 2-1 in 1997.

His trips in 2001, to Australia, and 2005, to New Zealand, when the Lions lost both times, were ended by serious injuries. A cruciate knee injury put paid to his tour to Australia and in New Zealand he broke his ankle in the tour opener against Bay of Plenty.

Dallaglio retired from international rugby after England's 2004 tour to New Zealand and Australia, but after regaining his appetite for the Test fray, he announced he would return in the winter of 2005, after successful ankle surgery.

England coach Andy Robinson didn't hesitate in bringing Dallaglio back for the 2006 Six Nations. He resumed his international career when coming off the bench against Wales, and plundered a charging trademark try – one of 16 five-pointers he has scored for his country.

In April 2006, Dallaglio signed a two-year extension to his contract at Wasps. By the time he put pen to paper, he had clocked up 285 club appearances, scoring 238 points.

"I'm delighted to have re-signed for the club, which means in effect that I'll finish my playing career where I started, at Wasps," he said.

"This club has always been about offering players the possibility of playing the best rugby they can, maximising their potential and opportunities."

Wasps director of rugby Ian McGeechan said: "Lawrence is one of the giants of the English and world game. He has proved himself an inspirational leader at Wasps over a long period, and combined that with exceptional professionalism in his approach and preparation as a player."

JOHN**EALES**

Name: John Anthony Eales
Born: 27 June 1970
Country: Australia
Position: Lock
Debut: 22 July 1991 v Wales
Caps: 86
Points: 173

Finding tributes about John Eales is perhaps the easiest job around, so glowing was everyone – from team-mates and rivals to mentors and even politicians – about the man they call 'Nobody', as in 'nobody's perfect'. His decade-long international career generated countless column inches, right to the very end when the gangly lock bowed out with a last-gasp 29-26 win over the All Blacks to retain the 2001 Tri-Nations title. Cue the plaudits, beginning with John O'Neill, then chief executive of the Australian Rugby Union.

"There is no more significant player in the history of the game," he said. "We've been fortunate in Australia to have many great players and many great captains, but I think the combination of great player, great captain and great person is pretty unique."

The coaches were equally effusive. "Rugby has a great custodian in John Eales," said Rod Macqueen, who stepped down as Wallabies coach six weeks before Eales retired. "It has been my pleasure to see him develop into a great captain."

"We're grateful for the legacy he's left," agreed Eddie Jones, Macqueen's successor, while John Connolly, Eales's long-time Queensland coach, once quipped: "John Eales would see the good side of Hannibal Lector."

But it wasn't just the rugby public who owed a debt of gratitude. John Howard, the Australian prime minister, reflected the feelings of the nation when he said:

"I wish to record my admiration for the magnificent contribution that John Eales has made to the game of rugby, and to Australian and international sport. He has been an inspirational leader, an outstanding and courageous player, and an example to all in the way he has conducted himself on and off the field."

It wasn't just good manners and sportsmanship that put Eales at the top end of rugby's long list of legends, however; as a player, he was exceptional. Playing for the Brothers club, he was called up by Queensland in 1990 and with the retirement of incumbent Bill Campbell made a second-row spot his own – eventually making 112 appearances for the state. The following year, he made his Wallaby debut in a 63-6 cakewalk against Wales in Brisbane, then starred in a 40-15 trouncing of England. His performance prompted All Blacks legend Colin Meads to predict: "He could be anything, and a force at this level for ten years."

What made Eales special was that he combined the traditional skill set of a second-row with the handling and kicking ability of a fly-half. During his international career, he kicked 31 conversions and 34 penalties which, when added to his two tries, gave him 173 Test points – putting him eighth on the all-time Wallaby point-scorer list as they began their 2006 programme.

In the Super 12 with Queensland Reds he was even more prolific, racking up 402 points from six tries, 66 conversions and 80 penalties – a record never bettered by a forward in the competition. Over the years his kicking for the Wallabies secured several tight contests, none more so than the 24-23 win over New Zealand in 2000, when Eales, with his principal goalkicker Stirling Mortlock having been substituted, took responsibility for a stoppage-time penalty kick in the swirling Wellington breeze. The Bledisloe Cup and, effectively, Australia's first Tri-Nations crown hinged on the outcome – and Eales coolly stroked the ball over from a wide angle.

It was his other talents that had impressed others early in his career, though – notably Rob Andrew, a man he stopped with a crucial try-saving tackle in the 1991 World Cup final at Twickenham. Wallaby coach Bob Dywer mused: "You tell me, how does a 6ft 7in second-rower run down a fleet-footed fly-half like Rob Andrew? As long as I live, I'll never know."

Eales's tackle helped earn Australia their first World Cup and the champions followed it up with their first Bledisloe Cup in 1992, a feat they had failed to achieve since 1986.

A shoulder injury meant Eales sat out 1993, but he was back for Australia's unsuccessful attempt to defend the world crown in 1995. The next year, Greg Smith handed Eales the captaincy. For the first time, things didn't go so smoothly as Australia were hammered 43-6 by New Zealand, losing successive Bledisloe Cup series by 2-0 and 3-0 and also being crushed 61-22 by South Africa (albeit without Eales).

LEFT
Eales on his way to winning the World Cup in 1991.

FAR LEFT
Eales was one of the finest lineout exponents the world has ever seen.

The defeats cost Smith his job and Macqueen took over, so creating a partnership that served as the catalyst for Australia's most trophy-laden era.

A 76-0 destruction of England during Clive Woodward's infamous 'Tour of Hell' in 1998 gave the world some idea of the Wallaby force that was emerging. And they backed up that slaughter with a 3-0 Bledisloe Cup win the same year.

The high point, however, was to come in 1999 when Eales's men romped through the 1999 World Cup, conceding just one try in six matches. The cup was secured with a 35-12 final win over France, giving Eales his second World Cup winners' medal and Australia a place in the record books as the only side to win the greatest rugby show on earth twice.

Still he wasn't finished. That nerveless kick brought the Bledisloe Cup in 2000 and paved the way for successive Tri-Nations titles. The icing on the cake for Eales's supreme career came in 2001. Nobody had ever led an Australia side to a series victory against the Lions and so it was left to 'Nobody' to do just that. Graham Henry's Lions – complete with Eales's great English rival Martin Johnson – came, saw and were conquered 2-1 by the Wallabies. "That was the last frontier, something no Australian team had managed to achieve," said Eales, who captained Australia a record 55 times.

One more Tri-Nations title later, Eales retired and the New Zealanders celebrated.

GARETH**EDWARDS**

Name: Gareth Owen Edwards
Born: 12 July 1947
Country: Wales
Position: Scrum-half
Debut: 1 April 1967 v France
Caps: 53
Points: 88

BELOW
Edwards after receiving a golden boot at the Painter's Hall, London, for his performance in the Five Nations tournament, 1978.

When Gareth Edwards scored his legendary try against Scotland in 1972, comedian Spike Milligan suggested that a church should be built where he started his run and a cathedral where he finished it, at Cardiff Arms Park. His score and the reaction to it were typical of the way Edwards was revered throughout the rugby world. To most people who saw him play it was simple: Gareth Edwards was the greatest player the world had seen!

On that unforgettable day against Scotland, Edwards, who had already given Wales the lead with a try, burst around the blind side of a scrum inside his own half. He kicked over full-back Arthur Brown and then hacked the ball left-footed into the mud-splattered in-goal area.

Cliff Morgan was in no doubt about Edwards's status. "Of all the players I've seen around the world, he was undoubtedly the greatest," said the former Wales and Lions fly-half. "He could have been a world star in almost any position – scrum-half, fly-half, centre, wing, full-back. He was a genius."

Edwards's try against Scotland was one of 20 he scored in the red of Wales but he scored an even more famous one in 1973 in a Barbarians shirt. Phil Bennett started the move close to his own try-line with a couple of dazzling sidesteps and the ball passed thrillingly through a number of hands before Derek Quinnell fed Edwards, who sprinted up the left flank and dived spectacularly over the line.

Edwards won a then world-record 53 caps for Wales and remarkably those caps – from his debut as a teenager against France in 1967 – were won in consecutive matches over an 11-year period. Edwards was never dropped – the proposition would have been ludicrous!

Edwards only failed to complete one of those games, getting injured in Wales' win over England in 1970 at Twickenham. He was forced off the field with 20 minutes remaining, to be replaced by

Chico Hopkins. Maesteg's Hopkins ended up scoring the crucial try, but there was never any doubt Edwards would be on duty for the next game.

Edwards stood like a colossus over arguably the most successful period in the history of Welsh rugby. With Edwards at the helm, Wales won an incredible three Grand Slams, five Triple Crowns, five outright championships and two shared titles, taking the rugby world by storm.

The son of a miner, he became Wales' youngest ever captain, at 20, when he led the side out in 1968 against Scotland and he went on to skipper the side 14 more times.

Even those who saw him in his early teens said he was a genius. Rugby teacher Bill Samuels was the first to spot his potential and was the man Edwards always saw as his mentor. Samuels encouraged him to go to the famous sporting school Millfield, where he was joined by JPR Williams. Attending Millfield allowed Edwards to enjoy a number of sports and his prowess at gymnastics was credited for some of the skill he showed on the rugby field.

Edwards's partnership with Barry John was made in heaven, according to Welsh rugby fans, who saw them play together 23 times. Edwards's superb passing and tactical understanding gave John the space to rule the roost from outside-half. But Edwards was also a supreme athlete, equally adept at shrugging off forwards to score a short-range try or showing opponents a clean pair of heels with a lung-bursting break.

Edwards's fame was also based on his role in another red jersey, that of the British & Irish Lions. Arguments rage about whether the 1971 or 1974 Lions team was the best ever, but to Edwards it hardly matters as he was the ever-present Test scrum-half on both tours.

Before 1971 the Lions were largely a team of glorious sport-ing losers, but the heroics of that summer – the 2-1 Test-series victory, with one draw, and an amazing record in New Zealand of won 22, lost one and drawn one – changed the way that the side was perceived, and Edwards was at the forefront.

John Dawes was Edwards's captain in 1971 and he remembers the great man with affection. "Gareth was the best athlete ever to play rugby football," Dawes says. "He'd never play unless he was in 100% condition and when he was at his peak he was almost unplayable."

Since retiring, Edwards has stayed close to the game as a commentator, as a columnist with the Western Mail and as a director at Cardiff rugby club. He has worked for the BBC and S4C, commentating for the latter in Welsh, his mother tongue.

In Who's Who, he lists fishing as one of his hobbies, and even wrote a book on the subject, appearing in the BBC series The Fishing Race.

He also enjoys shooting. In an interview, he once said he loved "putting on a dirty pair of trousers and going fishing or taking a gun into the fields. I do have an ideal place to live, somewhere where I can do my shooting and fishing."

He was awarded an MBE (though, many ask, why not a knighthood?) at the age of just 27, becoming the youngest rugby player to receive such an honour at that time.

ABOVE
Edwards takes on the All Blacks.

MIDDLE
Gareth Edwards of The Lions is tackled by New Zealand's Alan McNaughton, 1971.

FAR LEFT
Gareth Edwards in action during The Lions tour of South Africa, 1974.

SEAN
FITZPATRICK

Name: Sean Brian Thomas Fitzpatrick
Born: 4 June 1963
Country: New Zealand
Position: Hooker
Debut: 28 June 1986 v France
Caps: 92
Points: 55

During the inaugural World Cup in 1987, an audible groan could be heard across the host nation, New Zealand, when it was announced that captain Andy Dalton had been injured during training early in the tournament. But such was the impact of his young replacement, one Sean Brian Thomas Fitzpatrick, that even though Dalton regained his fitness by the knockout stage, he failed to regain his place.

"When I made my debut in 1986, I was a young kid and just happy to learn from Andy Dalton," Fitzpatrick recalled. "But unfortunately he got injured just before the first game of the World Cup. So I ended up playing all six games and for me it was just incredible to be part of a World Cup-winning side."

That surprise World Cup adventure was part of the most prolific career in All Blacks history. Until his 92-cap record was eclipsed by Jason Leonard, Fitzpatrick was the most capped forward in the history of the game. He is still the most capped hooker.

Fitzpatrick was a natural leader, and a man who commanded the highest respect amongst his rivals and team-mates.

He skippered New Zealand a record 51 times, 41 of which brought victories, and after appearing in that first World Cup, played in the next two as well, reaching the semi-finals in 1991 and then the final in 1995, when he was captain.

His run as skipper coincided with him breaking another record as he played in a remarkable 63 consecutive Test matches, a sequence that was only broken when he was rested, and left on the bench, for a World Cup pool match against Japan in 1995.

Fitzpatrick made his debut as a 23-year-old in 1986, as part of the 'Baby Blacks' side that took on France. The side was so called because the heart of the New Zealand team had been ripped out following the decision of a number of All Blacks to go on a rebel Cavaliers tour of South Africa. That decision led to a number of players being banned, giving Fitzpatrick his chance.

As a record-breaking captain, and despite the fact that New Zealand failed to win a World Cup under his leadership, his qualities were unrivalled, friends and foe alike recognising his special character. He had a number of front-row partners, but the most prolific combination was with Craig Dowd and Olo Brown, the three of them playing 34 Tests together – a New Zealand record.

He was a mobile forward, often giving opponents the feeling that there were four back-row forwards on the pitch, and he was also one of the best lineout throwers in the world. More than anything, though, he possessed a hardness, both physical and mental, that made him an opponent to be feared.

"He had an almost indefinable X factor of which all great All Black captains are made," said Laurie Mains, his coach in the early 1990s. "Following the tour to Australia in 1992 it was obvious he was something special."

A prop in his early days, winning Auckland honours at Under-16 and Under-18 level, he was a slow starter, not making his school first XV until he was in the sixth form. It was current All Blacks coach Graham Henry who moved him to the centre of the front row. "He was apprehensive at first, but I thought he was better equipped to play at hooker," said Henry.

His father, Brian, was also an All Black, playing 22 Tests between 1951 and 1954.

Many would see the 1987 World Cup victory or the series win over the 1993 Lions as Fitzpatrick's finest hour, but the man himself picks out a victory in 1996, appreciating one of the sport's greatest rivalries.

"In terms of rugby for the purist, for us New Zealanders beating South Africa is always so important," he explained. "We had never won a tour on South African soil, so to do that in 1996 was sensational.

"To see grown All Blacks of 70 or 80 years old crying when we got back and saying, 'Thank you so much for achieving it before I died' was very memorable. That meant a lot to me and being the captain of the team was quite amazing. We don't tour at the moment so it may never happen again."

Not only was Fitzpatrick involved in that historic series win, but in the same year he was a key component of the Auckland Blues side that won the first-ever Super 12 competition.

The triumph against the Springboks was a precursor to the first Tri-Nations series, as the game became professional. The All Blacks were to be the first winners.

A year later he was repeating the trick, again lifting the Tri-Nations, Super 12 and Bledisloe Cup trophies before the sun set on his career.

A colossus of the game, Fitzpatrick battled on bravely against injury towards the end of his career, but was forced to admit defeat in 1997, playing his last Test, as a substitute, against Wales at Wembley.

He scored the last of his 12 Test tries – a phenomenal total for a hooker – against Argentina in 1997, while in 1987 he managed two in one game when New Zealand beat Australia 30-16 at Sydney.

He became the manager of the Auckland Blues for a short time, and was part of the management when they won the Super 12 in 2003. He also worked as a rugby consultant for the New Zealand union, with responsibility for player development.

He was awarded the New Zealand Order of Merit and also managed the New Zealand Colts side in 1999.

Today he works in the media. He has provided expert analysis for ITV, Sky and the BBC, and continues to air his forthright views as a columnist for The Sunday Times in England.

DAVE
GALLAHER

Name: David Gallaher
Born: 30 October 1873
Country: New Zealand
Position: Wing-forward/hooker
Debut: 15 August 1903 v Australia
Caps: 6
Points: 0

"In death, he acquired a mystique. His grave (in a war cemetery in Belgium) became a shrine." So wrote Terry McLean in New Zealand Rugby Legends. In a land full of rugby legends, the Irish-born Gallaher was the forerunner of them all – the captain of the first-ever All Blacks touring side.

Originally from Donegal, he moved with his parents to New Zealand at a young age as part of Vesey Stewart's Ulster Plantation. Initially working farmland in Katikati, Bay of Plenty, his mother was the town's first teacher and the main source of income for a family of ten. Three years after she died, Gallaher moved to Auckland at the age of 17. It was a decision that would ultimately lead to him becoming a legend, as it was here that he made his name with Ponsonby rugby club.

Winning the Auckland senior championship with Ponsonby in 1897, he played 26 matches for Auckland between 1896 and 1909 – despite missing the best part of two seasons due to his service in the Boer War as a corporal in the Mounted Rifles.

His record of six caps does scant justice to his input into New Zealand rugby. At the beginning of his career, international rugby was at the embryonic stage and Gallaher turned out on six occasions for New Zealand (who hadn't even gained their 'All Black' moniker yet) prior to the country's first-ever International in 1903. Playing the likes of Wellington, New South Wales and Queensland, Gallaher and his team-mates notched up five wins from six games in the build-up to the country's inaugural Test match.

With Australia the opponents, New Zealand won 22-3 in Sydney and the legend was up and running. For his part, Gallaher began as a hooker before taking the controversial position of wing-forward or 'rover' as it was then called.

Great Britain offered the next Test opposition and were duly dispatched 9-3 in Wellington.

Gallaher's greatest achievement came with the first tour to Britain of the 'Originals'. Considering he'd not even been selected for the warm-up tour to Australia, his appointment as captain for the biggest tour in New Zealand rugby's brief history was a shock to many. In fact, so controversial was the decision that on the boat that sailed over he resigned, along with his vice-captain Bill Stead. The vote was put to the players and the pair were reinstated, although not with the kind of majority they'd have hoped for.

Those who had opted for Gallaher and Stead to remain in control were clearly right to do so, as the New Zealanders enjoyed phenomenal success on the marathon tour. Against

DAVE**GALLAHER**

the likes of Devon, Cornwall, Gloucester, Oxford University and Bedford, the Kiwis ran in try after try to record cricket-style scorelines.

Before the first Test was even played, Gallaher had already captained his side to 14 wins over various club and regional sides, and the tourists' innovative and dynamic brand of rugby proved too strong for Scotland and England, beaten 12-7 and 15-0 respectively.

It was during the tour that the 'All Blacks' nickname was coined. How it actually came about remains uncertain – one theory is that it was due to a description of them playing like 'all backs', while another centres on the colour of their strip – but either way it was thanks to Gallaher and his team that the New Zealand rugby side gained its famous alias.

Perhaps inevitably, it was the one defeat on New Zealand's pioneering tour that accrued most publicity. The team lost 3-0 to Wales in Cardiff in a game that attained legendary status for the controversial disallowing of a Bob Deans try, which would have squared the match. The Originals had won 27 successive tour games up to the Wales defeat, and they saw off all subsequent opponents, including Cardiff and Swansea, to complete the British leg of the tour. France provided the next opposition – in what was to be Gallaher's final International –

but couldn't get close to the All Blacks as they crumbled 38-8 in Paris.

Two more standard routs of British Columbia followed in North America and the tour was over. Gallaher had captained his side in 26 tour matches – he missed the Ireland Test, won 15-0, due to injury – and they had lost just once. The full tour record was: played 35, won 34, lost one; points for 976, against 59. They scored 243 tries, seven per match, and cruised to victory in nearly all their games.

The position occupied by Gallaher of wing-forward was the cause for much concern to the home sides. He was a big player for the era and his no-nonsense approach to the game provoked criticism from the local hacks, forcing him to respond by saying: "I must confess that the unfair criticism to which I have been subjected, while in Wales especially, has annoyed me."

Retiring from playing following the mammoth tour, Gallaher penned The Complete Rugby Footballer with his vice-captain Stead. That they had the knowledge to create such a book helped to explain why the New Zealanders were so far ahead of the world in a game that was created in the fields of England on the other side of the world.

Individuals were shaping the path of New Zealand rugby and Gallaher was one of them.

He went on to become a selector with Auckland for ten years from 1906 and took on the same role with the national side from 1907 until 1914 and the onset of World War One.

With his age taking him beyond the realms of conscription, Gallaher nonetheless volunteered to serve and he died during action in Belgium, aged 43.

In memory of one of their greats, the Auckland union created the Gallaher Shield, a trophy awarded to the best side within the premier club competition.

MIKE**GIBSON**

Name: Cameron Michael Henderson Gibson
Born: 3 December 1942
Country: Ireland
Position: Centre / Fly-Half
Debut: 8 February 1964 v England
Caps: 69
Points: 112

When John Dawes, captain of the 1971 Lions and coach of some of the great Wales teams of the Seventies, stops to pronounce on a player, then you sit up and take notice. So when Dawes described Mike Gibson, the Irish lawyer from Belfast, as "the complete player", it was high praise indeed. And Dawes, of course, would know, having played with Gibson in the midfield on the 1971 tour to New Zealand, and coached him with the Lions in 1977.

"Mike could run, pass, tackle, kick, you name it," said Dawes. "He had a long career but never played in an outstanding Irish team, so in 1971, among great players, he could show how good he really was. And he did, reaching extraordinary heights."

Gibson, a Cambridge University graduate, was prolific with the Lions, going on five tours in the famous red jersey and being part of the team that rewrote rugby history with a series win in New Zealand in 1971.

And he was no less revered with Ireland, playing 69 Tests for them, in addition to his 12 Tests for the Lions, during a career that spanned 15 years at the highest level.

His 40 caps at centre and 21 at fly-half for Ireland, out of his total of 69, showed his versatility, and it made him the country's most capped player until Leinster's Malcolm O'Kelly went past his famous mark in 2005.

His final Ireland Test came in 1979, when he played a big role in back-to-back victories over the Wallabies at the age of 36. He ended with a win and also started with one, for his debut in 1964 saw Ireland victorious at Twickenham for the first time in 16 years.

Willie Duggan was amazed by Gibson's performance in Gibson's final match in Sydney, as he remembers in David Walmsley's Lions of Ireland. "I wouldn't be a great one for congratulating people on their performances – I've never done that in my life – but the second Test Mike Gibson played for Ireland in Australia in 1979 was absolutely unbelievable," said Duggan. "You would not believe an individual could do so much. It was the first time I ever crossed the dressing room to shake someone's hand."

Irish Lion Sean Lynch added: "Mike Gibson was the jewel in the Lions' crown; he was just magic. He had everything you could ask for: speed, ability and he knew how to handle a ball. He could dummy-run, scissors, beat a man on the outside or inside, and he could read a game very well, too."

But it was with the Lions that Gibson, who played for Dublin University and Wanderers, earned his worldwide reputation and particularly with the 1971 tour party that returned as rugby immortals.

The first of Gibson's record-breaking Lions tours came in 1966, when Mike Campbell-Lamerton's side suffered a 4-0 whitewash in New Zealand, after going unbeaten in eight games in Australia. Even then, just two years after his Ireland debut, he was singled out for praise by All Blacks captain Wilson Whineray.

"I believe a team should play to its strengths," said Whineray, after seeing Gibson operate outside Welshman Dai Watkins, "and the Lions' greatest strength was their backs. Their outstanding back was Mike Gibson, who played 19 out of 25 games in New Zealand."

On his second Lions tour in 1968, Gibson showed his versatility and he did it with a record to boot, becoming the first replacement in international rugby. He ended up playing 11 of the 13 matches on tour after Barry John was forced out with injury.

A quicksilver centre for most of his career, Gibson was thrust into the outside-half jersey in 1968, an experience that looked to have stayed with him, and taught him a great deal for the rest of his career.

By the time the next tour came round in 1971, Gibson was in perfect harmony with John and Dawes, as they formed the midfield axis that helped deliver an historic series win, the only one in New Zealand in the history of the Lions.

"It was enriching to play in a side that had so much ability," said Gibson of that experience. "The three midfield men were all of one mind and when Barry had the ball, I tried to think in terms of something seemingly impossible or unorthodox and then got into that position."

The perception of Gibson's influence on the 1971 side has diminished in some quarters through the years, but those close to the trip always acknowledge how crucial he was. Barry Coughlan, the Irish Examiner's rugby correspondent, remembers Gibson's abilities in his book, Irish Lions 1896-2001.

"The general consensus was that Gibson was the man of the tour," said Coughlan, which considering some of the names on the trip was some statement. 'The Complete Footballer' ran a headline in a newspaper following the 47-9 thrashing of Wellington. Gibson's acceleration and deadly changes of direction were the main reason why Wellington were so devastated."

Gibson's fourth Lions tour came in 1974 and because he initially made himself unavailable for selection, only to replace the injured Alan Old towards the end of the trip, he failed to break into the Test side.

Gibson's Lions swansong arrived in 1977 when he made a record-breaking fifth trip with the famous tourists – only Willie John McBride has managed the same number.

Bill McLaren, the legendary Scottish commentator, believes Gibson had it all, from tactical astuteness to wonderful hands and an ability to punt onto a sixpence if he had to. "He's the most complete, all-round footballer I've ever seen," said McLaren. "He had a nose for a score. If there was a score going, you could bet your bottom dollar that CMS Gibson would be on the end of it. Although he looked skinny, he tackled like the crack of doom."

Gibson was awarded an MBE for his services to the game and was inducted into the International Rugby Hall of Fame in 1997.

GEORGE
GREGAN

Name: George Musarurwa Gregan
Born: 19 April 1973
Country: Australia
Position: Scrum-half
Debut: 18 June 1994 v Italy
Caps: 127
Points: 99

When George Gregan lined up in Marseille for the Test against France on 5 November 2005, his place as one of the immortals in rugby history was guaranteed. On that day, Gregan won his 115th international cap, overtaking Jason Leonard's haul for England, and making him the most capped player for a single country in the history of the game.

"It's been a very enjoyable ride," said Gregan, after passing Leonard's mark. "It doesn't seem so long ago that I was starting my Test career. And I'm still enjoying it, that's the main thing."

Eddie Jones, his national coach at the time, had also worked with him at the Brumbies and knew the player better than almost anyone.

"As captain, George is our foremost leader," said Jones. "He is at the fulcrum of everything we do, a world-class player, a total professional, an outstanding captain. That's why he's so important."

Born in Zambia, Gregan moved to Australia with his family when still a baby, settling in Canberra, a move that was not only fortuitous for the ACT Brumbies but for the whole of Australia. But perhaps we shouldn't be surprised by his record-breaking career as his unusual middle name – Musarurwa – means 'the chosen one'.

In Canberra, Gregan attended St Edmunds College, starting a career that not only spanned the amateur and professional eras but one in which he won every honour the game has to offer: World Cup, Super 12, Tri-Nations, Bledisloe Cup and Test series win over the Lions in 2001.

He has become renowned for his elusive running and bullet-like pass, not to mention his leadership as Wallabies captain, but it was his superb defence that first got him noticed on the international stage. Winning his fourth cap for Australia, he burst on to the Test scene with an astonishing tackle to deny All Black Jeff

Wilson in the 1994 Bledisloe Cup clash in Sydney, Wilson spilling the ball as a result and allowing the Wallabies to snatch a 20-16 victory.

Gregan's leadership skills set him apart and in 1997 he was made vice-captain of Australia, having to wait until the great John Eales retired in 2001 to step up to the captaincy itself.

That captaincy took him through the good times and the bad for the Wallabies and in November 2005, when he ran out against Wales, Gregan passed a significant milestone, captaining Australia for the 50th time, second only at the time to Eales, with 55.

"He doesn't need to change anything," explained Wallaby team-mate David Giffin when Gregan took

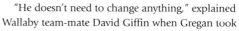

over the captaincy. "His playing position as a scrum-half puts him right in the thick of the action. He has good contact with the forwards and the backs, so that's an ideal place to lead from. George has the advantage of being a good communicator, as I discovered while playing under him at the Brumbies.

"His appointment also speaks volumes of the respect in which he is held by the game's administrators and the rapport that he has with them. Liaising between the team and the administrators is an important part of the skipper's role. The officials have shown their faith in his ability to do that."

In the 12 seasons he has played international rugby, up to 1 June 2006, he has missed just 13 Test matches for Australia. That run included a World Cup winner's medal in 1999, Gregan playing in every match in that tournament bar the pool game against USA, when most of the experienced Wallabies were rested.

Gregan was at his best in the 1999 World Cup. He crossed the try-line twice as Australia moved into the semi-finals with a 24-9 victory over Wales – two of 17 Test tries he has registered, alongside three drop-goals. And in the final against France he featured heavily in both tries as Australia cantered home 35-12.

That World Cup success in 1999 was followed by the agony of defeat four years later, the Wallabies losing to a last-minute drop-goal by England's Jonny Wilkinson.

But Gregan's humility at the end won him many friends. "It was an epic match," Gregan said. "It was an amazing game to be involved in and I am speaking on behalf of all the Wallaby players and management.

"We put everything into the campaign and came within a whisker of pulling it off. It certainly hurts and always will, but the effort from everyone makes me immensely proud. England deserved the victory and it confirmed what they had shown in the past three seasons.

"I always think that if you are the champion then someone has to come out and prove they are better than you when it counts – England proved this to me."

Gregan has established several commercial interests outside of rugby and has ploughed a great deal of time and energy into raising the awareness of epilepsy, after his son Max was diagnosed with the condition in 2005. With his wife Erica, Gregan has established the George Gregan Foundation, a project aimed at building playgrounds for sick children in hospital. The couple also established a chain of coffee shops in Sydney. Gregan is a national patron for Brainwave and received the Order of Australia for services to rugby in 2004.

In 2006 he started his 11th season with the Brumbies as one of only two foundation players left at the club and the only one to have reached the 100-game milestone. With Gregan only one cap behind Leonard's world record 119-cap haul (five of them gained with the Lions), the Australian is set to end his career out on his own – a fitting tribute to a very special talent.

GAVIN
HASTINGS

Name: Andrew Gavin Hastings
Born: 3 January 1962
Country: Scotland
Position: Full-back
Debut: 18 January 1986 v France
Caps: 61
Points: 667

People should have known something special was about to happen when they saw Gavin Hastings's performance in his first Test for Scotland. The man who had just led Cambridge University into the 1985 Varsity Match was thrown from the student arena into a Five Nations clash with France at Murrayfield. Hastings rose to the occasion magnificently, launching one of the greatest careers in British rugby with six penalties as Scotland prevailed 18-17. He went on to claim a then championship record of 52 points as the Scots shared the title.

Hastings never looked back from that stunning introduction, breaking records and setting new marks across the world. Scotland's leading point-scorer (667) and the man who has kicked more points in the World Cup Finals (227) than anyone else, he was the heartbeat of the Scotland side for almost a decade.

Even before his time at university, or that start against France, he had been earmarked as a future international, captaining the Scotland schoolboys to their first win over England.

Hastings went on to win 61 caps for Scotland – the last 20 of them as captain – as well as winning six caps for the Lions on the 1989 and 1993 tours. On those tours he scored more Test points (66) for the Lions than any other player, but it was the second of the trips, to New Zealand, in which he showed his mettle, courageously ignoring an injured hamstring to captain the Lions to victory in the second Test.

The highlight of his career, however, was Scotland's 1990 Grand Slam triumph, when the Scots sent Murrayfield wild by upsetting favourites England to clinch their second clean sweep in six years.

That Slam was followed by a 21-18 defeat in Auckland, Hastings taking Scotland closer than they've ever been to beating the All Blacks when he kicked two penalties from inside his own half and converted both tries to give Scotland an 18-12 half-time lead.

Captaincy seemed to come easy to Hastings and by the end of his career he had skippered Watsonians, Cambridge University, London Scottish, the Barbarians, Scotland and the Lions.

In Australia in 1989, he and Scott became the first brothers to appear in the same Lions Test team, since Tuan & Jack Jones (Wales) in 1908, and together they managed to turn the vital Test towards the Lions. With the Lions 1-0 down, Gavin scored the try in the second Test that put the tourists in front for the first time with just five minutes left, diving over the line following a pass from Scott. Concussed earlier in the game, he had

GAVIN**HASTINGS**

no recollection of scoring after the match, having to use a television replay to jog his memory.

Four years later Hastings was in magnificent form, but couldn't stop New Zealand turning the tables with a 2-1 series victory themselves. This time he eclipsed his 1989 record with 101 points on the whole tour, 12 of which came in that dramatic second Test when the Lions racked up their biggest ever win over New Zealand, 20-7, in Wellington.

Clem Thomas, in his definitive history of the Lions, summed up Hastings's influence in the famous red shirt, and why coach Ian McGeechan gave him the captaincy when the pressure back home was on to award it to England's Will Carling, who had led his side to consecutive Grand Slams in 1991 and 1992. "There is no man more respected for his abilities both on and off the field than this delightful Scot, who is the epitome of the rugby man; brave, resolute, adventurous and one who loves a party," wrote Thomas.

The narrow defeat the 1993 Lions suffered reflected well when you consider the 3-0 hammering handed out by the All Blacks when the Lions made their next visit, in 2005.

As skipper, Hastings could do no more, including the individual record of 18 points in a Test, scored in Christchurch, but in a titanic series the Lions came up short.

In 1993 he scored more points, 35, in a Lions Test series than anyone had done before him.

In Lions terms he followed an illustrious list of Scottish full-backs that included Andy Irvine and, from an earlier era, greats such as Ken Scotland and Stewart Wilson.

But not everything went to plan for Hastings. In the 1991 World Cup semi-final at Murrayfield, he missed a simple kick with the score at 6-6 – and Rob Andrew then put England through with a drop-goal. Hastings was criticised when he and his team-mates turned up for the final at Twickenham wearing the colours of England's opponents, Australia.

Hastings's World Cup debut in 1987 had started far more brightly, as he scored 27 points against Romania and 19 against Zimbabwe. But a 20-20 draw against France set them up for a quarter-final with hosts New Zealand that was lost 30-3.

He retired after the 1995 World Cup after the Scots were again knocked out in the last eight by New Zealand, this time by 48-30. That game was his 61st and final capped appearance for Scotland, a record that was later surpassed by brother Scott.

Hastings has stayed immersed in sport, helping to manage the Scotland sevens side and establishing Hastings International, which he set up with Scott. The company has continued with a wide brief and it ensured Hastings was behind projects such as the Scottish Ryder Cup bid, which resulted in Gleneagles being awarded the venue for 2014, as well as consulting on the women's Solheim Cup, which came to Loch Lomond in 2000.

Hastings's full-time move into the business world didn't come until a brief flirtation with American Football, and he helped the Scottish Claymores to victory in the World Bowl at Murrayfield.

His contribution to rugby was recognised with an OBE in the 1994 New Year's Honours List.

LEFT
Hastings, in action for his beloved Scotland, at Murrayfield.

FAR LEFT
As captain of the Lions in 1993.

NEIL**JENKINS**

Name: Neil Roger Jenkins
Born: 8 July 1971
Country: Wales
Position: Fly-half
Debut: 19 January 1991 v England
Caps: 87
Points: 1,049

In the sport of rugby there have been good goalkickers, great goalkickers and then there's the lad from Church Village in South Wales, Neil Jenkins. Jenks to everyone in the Principality, he became one of the true greats of Welsh rugby through his exploits with the boot.

Affectionately named the Ginger Monster, when he retired from Test rugby in 2002 he was Wales's most capped player and the world-record holder for points scored in Internationals. He scored a mammoth 1,049 points for Wales and a further 41 in four Tests for the British & Irish Lions.

In the 1999 World Cup against Samoa, he passed Michael Lynagh's previous world-record mark of 911 points and he then became the first player in the history of the game to score 1,000 Test points.

Capped at just 19, remarkably he took only 28 Tests to become Wales's leading point-scorer.

Rugby fans seemed to enjoy Jenkins's success later in his career, mainly because of the way he suffered in the early days. As Welsh rugby struggled to live up to the trophy-laden 1970s, Jenkins was made the scapegoat for a struggling side.

But within the game, his true worth was recognised. Lynagh, the man whose record he took, is a big fan. "Neil is more deserving of the record than I am because he has done it the hard way. For years he has been part of a Welsh team that struggled, whereas in my career for Australia we rarely had a dip in form," Lynagh said.

"At last he is getting the recognition he deserves as a player. He had to suffer taunts that he is only in the team because of his kicking. Neil is the best goalkicker around, but he would be in the Wales team even if he couldn't land a penalty from 15 yards."

It says much for his mental strength that Jenkins emerged from the dark days with some stunning performances for Wales,

BELOW
Jenkins was never too far away from an award like this Man of the Match accolade he won for Cardiff in 2000.

and he also produced a series of outstanding games as the Lions beat South Africa in 1997.

On that tour he was switched from outside-half to full-back, to accommodate Gregor Townsend at No 10, and it was his kicking exploits in the midweek side that helped turn the trip in favour of the Lions.

Everyone remembers the way Jeremy Guscott kicking the winning drop-goal in the second Test in Durban to clinch the series 2-0. But it was Jenkins who got them to that point with five penalties to ensure the score was 15-15 before Guscott got the chance to strike.

"I had never felt an atmosphere like the one in Durban before," Jenkins recalled. "When South Africa ran out I thought they were going to run right through the stadium at the other end, they were so up for it. They threw everything at us, but our defence was superb with Dallaglio and Gibbs tackling everything. How we won that match I will never know.

"My first cap against England in Cardiff in 1991 was the proudest sporting day of my life. But my greatest moment on a rugby field has to be playing with the triumphant Lions team in South Africa in 1997, particularly winning the second Test in Durban. Just awesome!"

In his autobiography Life at Number 10, Jenkins reveals how he started his working life before rugby became professional, being employed in the South Wales valleys as a scrap merchant prior to ending up as one of the most sought-after players in Britain.

His iconic status at his beloved Pontypridd probably helped him through the bad times with Wales, and he repaid them by helping the club to win the league title and the Principality Cup. He stayed at Pontypridd for 12 years, before moving to Cardiff.

Throughout his career he was a very modest man and it seems as though it was his passion for the Welsh shirt that helped him during the spells when the flak was flying.

"Putting on that red shirt means so much. It is difficult to explain the feeling unless people have actually done it. And for a Welshman the No 10 shirt is particularly special," Jenkins said.

As Welsh rugby changed, so did Jenkins and when many of Pontypridd's players were merged into the new (but now defunct) Celtic Warriors, Jenkins set a remarkable record. He was successful with 44 consecutive kicks for the Warriors, another world record.

"If someone had offered me this career when I was starting out, I would have ripped their arm off to take that and said thanks very much," Jenkins told Rugby World magazine. "I am pretty lucky."

He became an almost permanent fixture in the Wales side after making his debut in 1991 against England, his best moment in a Wales shirt coming eight years later in the same shirt.

Everyone remembers Scott Gibbs's try which 'defeated' England at Wembley in 1999, but Jenkins still had to hold his nerve to kick the conversion. It was actually Jenkins's kick that gave Wales their incredible 32-31 victory.

"After Scott Gibbs had scored his try, he just smiled at me, thrust the ball in my hands and said: 'Just kick the damn thing'. After that I was afraid to miss!" Jenkins said. "It was a fantastic day and we haven't beaten England very often in my career – that made it very special."

After retiring, Jenkins started working with the new Wales Academy.

BARRY**JOHN**

Name: Barry John
Born: 6 January 1945
Country: Wales
Position: Fly-half
Debut: 3 December 1966 v Australia
Caps: 25
Points: 90

It may seem strange that a player with only 25 caps and 90 points for his country could make the pantheon of rugby legends. But in the case of Barry John the statistics only tell a small part of the story. The George Best of rugby lit up the game in the early 1970s with a scintillating brand of rugby that led to him being considered the greatest talent of his generation.

"The one and only," is how John Dawes describes the Wales and Lions outside-half.

"His reading of the game, his knowledge, taking the right option, kicking off either foot, passing off either hand, gliding through on the break…"

Known simply in Wales as 'The King', John left a nation stunned when he retired in his prime at just 27. He was one of the first rugby players to move in celebrity circles and, according to his autobiography, The King, pressure was the biggest factor behind his departure.

It was in the red of Wales that we first heard the gasps at his skill and the looks of awe from the crowd, but it was in another red shirt where he enjoyed his finest hours – for the British & Irish Lions.

When the Lions arrived in New Zealand in 1971, it was on the back of an awful recent history, and without a series win over the All Blacks in their history. But with John pulling the strings and the side packed with his Welsh colleagues, the Lions won an unforgettable series, 2-1 with one draw, changing the course of rugby in both hemispheres.

"I could always see things early and that enabled me to claim my adversary's space before he knew it," John once said, "and I reckon you can over-analyse videos to the stage where you are frightened to attempt anything.

"Andy Irvine was pretty similar while Besty [George Best] was poetry in motion on a football pitch. Sure, we made plenty of mistakes, but I never worried about them. I was always looking ahead to the next move and working out that if I kept changing my angles of attack, and thinking off the cuff, I'd get more things right than wrong."

John played one Test for the Lions in 1968, but broke his collarbone as they lost to South Africa. It was a different story three years later.

"It wasn't just us who revered him, New Zealand did too," Dawes said after seeing John terrorise the All Blacks in their own backyard.

John played in all four Tests in New Zealand and made an impact that may never be matched. Under the guiding hand of coach Carwyn James, he not only registered a record 191 points in his 17 matches on that trip but scored 30 of the Lions' Test total of 48. Of course he had a touch of arrogance, but that is one reason he was loved across the world, and on that tour he taunted his rivals by sitting on the ball in protest at the foul play of Hawke's Bay.

Irish great Mike Gibson remembers John's influence only too well: "He was the name of the 1971 tour. His control of the game and his composure influenced all the other players. His brain operated at a speed that would allow him to do all the things he wanted to do.

"It's not something you would be aware of just viewing the match, but if you experienced playing with him, being in his company, he had a marked influence on players, even on the forwards, who had complete faith in what the back-line was going to do. In the most difficult circumstances he was in control."

No 8 Mervyn Davies saw a different side to John that shows why the No 10 was the coolest customer in the team. "On the Lions tour, we'd all be in the dressing room banging our heads against the wall, but Barry would be in such a relaxed state you'd think he was popping out for a stroll," recalled Davies. "He was so laid-back, he'd just tell us: 'Don't worry, boys, it's only a game. Just give me the ball and I'll win it. It's just the All Blacks; they're not supermen'."

John began his career at Llanelli but later joined Cardiff and linked up in irrepressible style with Gareth Edwards. It was a half-back partnership made in heaven.

John made his debut for Wales against Australia in December 1966, and less than a year later he paired up at Test level with Edwards for the first time, in the 13-6 defeat by New Zealand.

For most people 1971 means the Lions, but in the same year John had already scored a vital try for Wales against France to win the Grand Slam.

Rodney Webb, the man who developed the modern rugby ball, remembers John's incredible skill with the ball in hand. Webb, who also played for England, rates him as the greatest goalkicker of all time and added: "Barry John's punting was phenomenal. He could drop the ball on a sixpence and he could do it every time. He was a genius at reading a game as well, and his goalkicking was so accurate that he didn't just break all the records when the Lions toured in New Zealand in 1971, he smashed them."

John ended his career against France in Cardiff in 1972. He famously declined the chance to kick the final conversion, with Wales already in the clear.

"Rugby is about tries, so I handed the ball to Gareth [Edwards], walked off, kissed my boots and went home," John said. "Statistics didn't matter a damn. Never have, never will. As long as you can put a smile on people's faces, what more could you want?"

John put a smile on the faces of legions of rugby fans. We may have had him in our game for a short time, but the quality he brought will never be forgotten.

MARTIN
JOHNSON

Name: Martin Osbourne Johnson
Born: 9 March 1970
Country: England
Position: Lock
Debut: 16 January 1993 v France
Caps: 84
Points: 10

When England won the World Cup in 2003, it was the right boot of Jonny Wilkinson that delivered the Webb Ellis Cup to Twickenham. But the 20-17 victory over Australia was built on the blood, sweat and toil of every player, and none more so than their inspirational captain, Martin Johnson. So in many ways it was fitting that it was Johnson who took the ball up, gaining the hard yards in the move that led to Wilkinson's famous drop goal.

When he lifted the World Cup to a television audience of millions, it was his last act in an England shirt, as he retired from international rugby shortly after, at the age of 33. Great sportsmen always end on a high.

"You can't overestimate the impact he's had on the game – for club, country and for the British & Irish Lions," said Clive Woodward, the coach who oversaw that World Cup triumph. "Jonno is an awesome individual, a world-class player and his leadership is outstanding."

Former Ireland captain Keith Wood, who played with Johnson on two Lions tours, added: "As a leader he was the best captain I ever had. He would let his body and actions do all the talking. He was the most influential skipper I've encountered and as a player he will go down as one of the all-time greats."

The trophies, accolades and milestones arrived at regular intervals in Johnson's incredible career. He won every honour the game had to offer. When he retired from international rugby, he'd won 84 England caps – 39 of them as captain – and eight Lions caps in an 11-year career. Along the way he collected six Triple Crowns, five championship titles and two Grand Slams (1995 and 2003), as well as playing on three Lions tours, captaining two of them, including the against-the-odds triumph in South Africa in 1997.

In English senior rugby he was a one-club man, and after taking over the Leicester captaincy in 1997 he led them to four successive Premiership titles (1999-2002) and back-to-back European Heineken Cup triumphs in 2001 and 2002, plus a Pilkington Cup victory in 1997.

He also had time for a couple of trips to Buckingham Palace to meet the Queen and pick up both an MBE and a CBE.

He became the first man to captain the Lions on successive tours in 1997 and 2001, and his coach on the first trip, Ian McGeechan, summed up his influence.

"I just thought of him walking down the corridor, and the South Africans opening the changing-room door," said McGeechan. "They'd look up and see Jonno and know that we meant business."

But it so nearly wasn't to be. Johnson joined Leicester in 1989 but not before a year in New Zealand – where he met his wife-to-be Kay – and was selected for the New Zealand Under-21s tour of Australia. Many in New Zealand were desperate for him to stay and change his citizenship. Thankfully for England, he decided to return home after that sojourn.

His England debut followed in 1993 against France and the same year he flew out to replace Wade Dooley on the Lions tour of New Zealand.

Replacing Johnson at Leicester, England and the Lions was simply not an option. When they built Martin Johnson they broke the mould.

With him out of the England side – along with a few others – England went on a huge downward spiral, finishing well down the table in the three championships following his departure.

His Leicester team-mates were well aware of what they were losing when he packed up his boots. "We know Jonno is probably an impossible guy to replace," admitted his second-row colleague, Ben Kay. Tigers fly-half Andy Goode added: "Losing Jonno's leadership is huge. Not only that, he's the best player in his position in the world and has been for a number of seasons."

Martin Corry replaced him as Leicester captain, and eventually with England. "The important thing is that I don't try to copy Martin," said Corry after this appointment. "Sure, we both lead by example, but I don't have all his attributes, starting with his technical knowledge and captaincy experience."

Leading by example was Johnson's biggest strength, as his England colleague Jason Leonard remembers. "As a captain he would never ask one of his team-mates to do anything he wouldn't. He was a respected figure worldwide, and the complete competitor. He doesn't like to lose at anything and would never take a backward step. He would never avoid hard work – he always rolled up his sleeves and got stuck in."

LEFT
Johnson holds up The Calcutta Cup after defeating Scotland in the Six Nations match at Twickenham, 2001.

FAR LEFT
Johnson rises highest during a match between Australia and The Lions.

One of his finest matches came against the All Blacks in June 2003. With Lawrence Dallaglio and Neil Back in the sin-bin, England had to survive four successive scrums on their own line with a six-man pack. Johnson and his fellow forwards did it, enabling England to scrape a 15-13 win of huge psychological significance ahead of that year's World Cup. Asked afterwards what was going through his mind at the time, Johnson displayed his customary wit: "Nearly my spine."

His final game came fittingly at Twickenham when a Martin Johnson XV beat a Jonah Lomu XV in June 2005. "I'll walk away and won't be doing a George Foreman, although maybe I'll be selling toasters in four years' time!" said Johnson. "That was a brilliant way to go out. I was more emotional than I thought I'd be – I thought I'd just play and walk away. To get a crowd of 42,000 for a match like that is amazing."

In competitive terms, he ended on the losing side as Wasps beat Leicester 39-14 in the Premiership final a month before, his 500th first-class match.

Johnson is still living and breathing sport, raising thousands of pounds for SPARKS, a children's charity founded and supported by top names in sport and entertainment.

JACKIE**KYLE**

Name: John Wilson Kyle
Born: 10 January 1926
Country: Ireland
Position: Fly-half
Debut: 25 January 1947 v France
Caps: 46
Points: 24

**Since Ireland joined the Home International Championship – now the Six Nations –
in 1883, they have only managed one Grand Slam. In 2006 they came within a
victory over France of a clean sweep but, as many times before, the Grand Slam
slipped from their grasp.**

But in 1948 the Slam was theirs in a period of rugby history where the Irish
were pre-eminent.

That side had some memorable players, including captain Karl Mullen, but crucially
they had a fly-half from heaven, John Wilson Kyle, known throughout the rugby world
as Jackie.

Long before Lansdowne Road became the home of Irish rugby, Internationals were
regularly held at Ravenhill and 30,000 people packed it to the rafters to see the Grand
Slam won with a 6-3 victory over Wales.

Winning a Triple Crown in 1949 and the championship in 1951, to follow the Slam of
1948, ensured this was a golden era for Irish rugby.

Mullen was Kyle's captain in 1948 and he remembers his huge influence over the side.

"We discussed our tactics, and analysis of the Welsh team brought forth the conclusion
that they had some great players; mistakes must be cut to a minimum," said Mullen in
Ned Van Esbeck's Irish Rugby Scrapbook.

"Indeed, the ability to remain free from error at the crucial moments was a notable
characteristic of the Irish side of that period. Then we had Kyle, in my view incomparable
before and since. We decided to put our faith in our forwards and leave Kyle to play to
our strength. Kyle was the genius and the inspiration… In the closing stages Kyle was
magnificent as he sent the Welsh back time after time."

The 1948 Slam produced a number of tributes for Kyle and his team, but none more
appealing than the words of Irish rugby journalist Paul MacWeeney, who reconstructed
lines from the Scarlet Pimpernel:

They seek him here, they seek him there;

Those Frenchies seek him everywhere;

That paragon of graft and guile;

That dammed elusive Jackie Kyle!

Kyle himself remembers that time with understandable fondness, exposing a few
differences from modern-day rugby.

JACKIE**KYLE**

"The first game in 1948 was against France and it was on a Thursday – New Year's Day," he said. "With the game in the French capital, there was great excitement in the team as none of us had been there before.

"It was England next and an 11-10 victory. I was never so glad to hear the final whistle. The final game was something special. Back in my own home town, and as a 22-year-old student it was really something. I can remember being carried off. It was a real frenzy. Looking back on it now, it was a more remarkable occasion than any of us realised at the time."

Kyle's career was remarkable not just because of his ability; his longevity was something the game hadn't seen before, and when he finally retired in 1958, after an 11-season international career, it was with a then world-record 46 caps.

He had an incredible run in the Ireland team, playing in seven consecutive championship seasons without missing a game before injury removed him temporarily from the scene in 1954. When Ireland played England that season without Kyle in the ranks, it was the first game he had missed since the war.

He made his official Ireland debut against France in 1947, Ireland's first post-war game, and crowds were soon standing in awe of his elusive running and lightning speed off the mark, making him a nightmare for opponents to mark.

Kyle played his final game for Ireland in 1958, going out on a 12-6 win, and only a few weeks after he helped Ireland beat Australia 9-6.

The Little Book of **RUGBY** LEGENDS

He also captained Ireland on six occasions, in 1953 and 1954.

Kyle, who was inducted into the rugby Hall of Fame in 1999, also had an unforgettable Lions tour in 1950, when he played in all six Tests, four against New Zealand and two against Australia.

He played in 20 matches on that trip, scoring seven tries and prompting The Rugby Almanack of New Zealand to select him as one of its five Players of the Year. The almanack described him as "an excellent team man, faultless in his handling, able to send out lengthy and accurate passes, and adept at making play for his supports".

The Lions were unlucky to lose that series, drawing the first game 9-9 in Dunedin, where Kyle gave arguably his greatest performance for the tourists. That day he scored three of the Lions points with a try, then put in a famous punt to set up another score for Wales wing Ken Jones.

In John Griffiths's History of the British and Irish Lions, Kyle is remembered as a gentleman who seemed to win as many supporters off the field as he did on it.

"Renowned for his sportsmanship and unsurpassed technical ability, Kyle was portrayed at the time of his international retirement as typifying everything which is cherished in rugby union football," Griffiths said. "Few have subsequently matched his brilliance on the field; off the field, none has shown more gentlemanly or modest demeanour."

That spirit of rugby that coursed through Kyle's veins manifested itself in an incredible way in one nail-biting match against Wales. When Kyle went over in the corner and touched down, the referee awarded the try to trigger celebrations from the crowd and Kyle's team-mates. But once Kyle had picked himself up, he went over to the referee and told him that he had dropped the ball as he went over the line. The referee disallowed the try.

A surgeon by trade, Kyle trained at Queen's University Belfast, and once his rugby career was over he spent more than 30 years working in Africa.

LEFT
Kyle is chaired off the pitch after winning his 45th cap.

FAR LEFT
Kyle was a Lions legend.

JASON
LEONARD

Name: Jason Leonard
Born: 14 August 1968
Country: England
Position: Prop
Debut: 28 July 1990 v Argentina
Caps: 114
Points: 5

**When the 2003 World Cup final went into extra time, the only thing that was
going to stop England lifting the Webb Ellis Cup was the way they were struggling
to cope with referee Andre Watson. England had the upper hand over a weak
Australian front row, but Watson was consistently penalising them. So coach Clive
Woodward called on the most experienced rugby player in the history of the game,
Jason Leonard.**

In the semi-final against France, Leonard had passed Philippe Sella's previous world-
record haul of 111 caps, but now he was asked to produce his most telling performance.
And in the final Leonard immediately placated the irritated Watson and put a stop to the
penalties that England were conceding. It was a fitting end to one of the greatest careers
rugby has seen and, although he won one more cap in the Six Nations that followed, those
who know the game will always view his late intervention in Sydney as his curtain call.

Leonard was the only survivor from the 1991 final, when England had lost to Australia.
That 2003 World Cup was Leonard's fourth tournament, and by the end no player had
taken part in more matches in World Cup Finals than Leonard's 18.

He had already passed 100 caps earlier in the year and of the five players who had
broken the century by the end of the 2006 Six Nations, Leonard is the only one from the
unforgiving territory of the front row. It was in 1995 that he became England's most
capped prop, in his 38th Test, and a year later he became the youngest England player to
win 50 caps when taking the field against Italy at Twickenham.

The World Cup triumph was the pinnacle but before then Leonard had been involved
in four Grand Slam sides, in 1991, 1992, 1995 and 2003.

Try-scoring was certainly not his forte, although he did get over the line once, in 1996
during a 20-18 win against Argentina. He was captain that day, and received the honour
for a second time in 2003, when England played a World Cup warm-up against Wales.

Leonard started his front-row education at Barking, a carpenter by trade, moving to
Saracens and then to Harlequins, but his big break came in 1990. Leonard not only
made his Test debut in that year as a 21-year-old but it was in Argentina, where front-row
play is an art form. England's selectors knew that if Leonard could cope in Argentina then
he could cope anywhere.

And cope he did over an unprecedented career, making a seamless transition from
amateur to professionalism and, although he prospered on the field, he never forgot his

roots and how to enjoy the spirit of rugby.

With nicknames like 'The Fun Bus' and 'The Scourge of the Barking Barmaids', the stories in his autobiography, Jason, were legendary. In that tome he names his 'All-time drinking XV' from team-mates past and present, which sums up his fun-loving character.

He was one of the most popular players ever to grace the sport and this was summed up by his England colleague Jonny Wilkinson. "For any player, let alone a prop, to achieve 100 caps is a massive achievement," Wilkinson said. "All that and he's never missed an opportunity to walk out in an England shirt through injury. It's a record that is unlikelyto be bettered. He is one of the great heroes of the English game. He's renowned as someone who's always welcoming and he's always got a story to tell. It will be a massive blow, both to England and rugby in general, when he finally decides to hang up his boots."

Those boots were hung up in a competitive sense when he came on as substitute in the 2004 Challenge Cup final against Montferrand. At 35, Leonard appeared seven minutes from time after a 14-year, 219-match career. He bowed out in style – with more silverware – as Quins won 27-26.

Leonard was offered a further one-year contract with Quins but said: "I wanted to go out while I'm still playing good rugby. I still love the game and will miss the dressing-room banter and training sessions enormously. Being able to play for my country has been an honour and one I have never taken for granted. And I never did."

In that final season in 2004, then England coach Woodward made one of his few mistakes, failing to recognise that both Leonard and Neil Back had one more Six Nations campaign left in them. Woodward had already lost Wilkinson to injury and

Martin Johnson to retirement. Leonard's final Test appearance came off the bench against Italy in that Six Nations, though he did don an England shirt one more time, in the non-cap 32-12 defeat by the Barbarians in May 2004. He scored a try that day and received a standing ovation from the Twickenham crowd when leaving the field.

It wasn't just in the white of England where Leonard set new benchmarks for props, however, as he went on three successive Lions tours, in 1993, 1997 and 2001.

Leonard's career may have had many highs but it didn't all run smoothly, far from it. He appeared in 40 consecutive Tests between 1990 and 1995, an achievement made even more extraordinary because that sequence included an operation, in 1992, to repair ruptured vertebrae in his neck using bone taken from his pelvis. He was told he would never walk again after undergoing life-saving surgery, but in the event the operation hardly made him break stride as he marched towards legendary status. In 2002 Leonard was awarded an MBE for services to rugby, and an OBE followed in 2003.

JONAH**LOMU**

Name: Jonah Tali Lomu
Born: 12 May 1975
Country: New Zealand
Position: Wing
Debut: 26 June 1994 v France
Caps: 73
Points: 215

No player has made a bigger impact at a Rugby World Cup than Jonah Lomu. The game's first global superstar, the New Zealander burst onto rugby's greatest stage like a tornado during the third World Cup, in South Africa in 1995. England had arrived at the tournament as Grand Slam champions and one of the favourites for the title. Australia, the holders, had been dispatched in the quarter-finals, so Will Carling and his troops headed to Cape Town confident that they could overcome the All Blacks and take their place in the final for the second tournament running.

But Carling and Co hadn't reckoned on a giant winger who had only celebrated his 20th birthday one month before. Lomu took it upon himself to destroy the European champions with an astonishing four tries, most of them involving going round, through or over helpless Englishmen as if they were mere schoolboys.

His first came within four minutes of the kick-off. From the moment he trampled over full-back Mike Catt on his way to the line, everyone watching knew they were in the presence of greatness. Was this the most natural talent the game had seen?

"Jonah Lomu was the difference – a huge, huge difference," said Carling after England's somewhat flattering 45-29 defeat. "The All Blacks played amazing rugby, but the real difference appeared out on their left wing. We tried to stop him but we couldn't and that's very sad for us. But the man is unbelievable. He's very balanced, has that incredible power and anyone coming onto the ball like he did is almost impossible to stop."

That 1995 World Cup was to end in disappointment for the All Blacks as they succumbed to South Africa in the final, but nobody was in any doubt as to who was the star of the tournament. Lomu had stolen the show and he finished the leading try-scorer with seven tries in five matches.

Four years later it was almost the same story, as Lomu scored another long-range try of power and aggression to help beat England in a pool game at Twickenham. The try sent England into a quarter-final play-off and eventual elimination against South Africa.

New Zealand again failed to lift the Webb Ellis Cup in 1999, this time Australia taking the crown for a second time, but it wasn't for the want of trying on Lomu's part as he once more caused mayhem. The All Blacks crashed out to France in the semi-finals but not before Lomu had scored two tries in which numerous Frenchmen were swatted aside.

At 18st 12lb (120kg) and 6ft 5in (1.96m), Lomu was built for the forwards, but his speed (10.8 seconds for 100 metres) ensured that, to the dismay of international three-quarters everywhere, he ended up on the wing. At school his sprint training included running around the field pulling a lawn-roller with a rope tied around his waist.

The All Blacks were quick to spot Lomu's potential, though in truth it was hard to miss after he announced himself in spectacular style at the 1994 Hong Kong Sevens. Lomu, Eric Rush and Christian Cullen ran amok as New Zealand took the title with a 32-20 win over Australia in the final.

His prowess at sevens brought him a gold medal four years later as New Zealand triumphed at the 1998 Commonwealth Games in Kuala Lumpur.

Lomu also led New Zealand to victory at the 2001 Sevens World Cup, filling in for the injured Rush.

Once the privileged few had seen him in Hong Kong, it was only a matter of time before Lomu made his New Zealand debut. When that day arrived, against France in June 1994, Lomu was aged 19 years and 45 days – the youngest player to play a Test for the All Blacks.

Born in Auckland of Tongan descent, Lomu grew up in South Auckland and played rugby league up to the age of 14, when his parents sent him to Wesley College, a Methodist boarding school near Auckland.

He first came to the attention of the national selectors when playing for Counties Manukau in the NPC. His promotion followed swiftly, Lomu playing in the Super 12 for the Auckland Blues, Waikato Chiefs and Wellington Hurricanes.

Unfortunately for the game, Lomu was to be struck down in his prime after being diagnosed with nephrotic syndrome, a rare and serious kidney disorder that ultimately led to him having a transplant. The disease first surfaced in 1995, when he took antibiotics in an effort to control it.

John Mayhew, the New Zealand doctor, said in 1997: "The characteristics of this disease, caused by chronic kidney damage, is that he is suffering from low body protein in his blood. How he has managed to train and play I am not sure? We have been monitoring his condition and it has deteriorated markedly in that period of time." Remarkably, two years later Lomu was destroying England in the World Cup.

Eighteen months after his transplant, Lomu made a comeback in Britain, signing for Cardiff Blues in 2005 as he tried to get his career back on track against enormous odds.

Many people believed Lomu would never play again given the severity of his medical condition, and he needed special clearance from the World Anti-Doping Agency, as one of the drugs he was prescribed was on the list of banned substances.

But beat those odds he did and he made his first appearance in a competitive match since his transplant when, in December 2005, he played for Cardiff Blues against Calvisano in Italy.

By the end of the season, he was vowing to fight his way back into New Zealand's squad for the 2007 World Cup. An impossible challenge? Nothing, it seems, is beyond Jonah Lomu.

ABOVE
Lomu was a star on the Sevens circuit.

MIDDLE
Lomu on his way to demolishing England in the 1995 World Cup semi-final.

FAR LEFT
Lomu powers through against Wales, at Wembley Stadium.

WILLIE JOHN
MCBRIDE

Name: William James McBride
Born: 6 June 1940
Country: Ireland
Position: Lock
Debut: 10 February 1962 v England
Caps: 63
Points: 4

Rarely has one man encapsulated the spirit of something in the way that Willie John McBride did with the British & Irish Lions. In the same way that Gareth Edwards was the ultimate Barbarian thanks to that try, McBride is the ultimate Lion due to his remarkable leadership skills that united four nations to take on and inflict a crushing defeat upon one of the greatest forces in world rugby – the Springboks. Captaining a club side is one thing, captaining an international side is another, but to successfully bring together players from across the United Kingdom and Ireland and take them on a lengthy tour to the other side of the world is a totally different ball game.

Alun Thomas, the tour manager for the 1974 Lions, wrote of McBride: "His outstanding qualities as a player and a man are so well known that I can never adequately describe them in print. He was literally worshipped by the players, not only because of his own courage and strength of commitment, but because they saw in him all the things they would like to be. He shielded them, nurtured them and, above all, inspired them. He shirked nothing, and was that rare breed, a natural leader of men."

A Lions tourist on five occasions, McBride first pulled on the famous red shirt in 1962 when they toured South Africa. The tour was a failure in terms of results – the Lions lost three Tests and drew one – but it did mark the emergence of McBride, as full-back Tom Kiernan acknowledged in the book Lions Of Ireland: "Willie John wasn't expected to get a Test place but he ended up in the team for the last two Tests. He was a relative newcomer to rugby, so he was still immature, but his value in securing possession was pretty high even then."

Having not even touched a rugby ball until his late teens, McBride's rise to the top was phenomenal. He studied at Ballymena Academy, played for Ulster and then gained his first Ireland cap aged just 21 against England in a 16-0 loss at Twickenham.

Unfortunately for McBride, his international career coincided with some lean times with Ireland. In that first year, Ireland finished bottom of the Five Nations and while managing second place on four occasions during his career, they would win the title just once – in 1974. At the peak of his powers and just a few months before the Lions tour that would make him a household name, McBride led Ireland to their first crown in 23 years.

Yet the men in green didn't have the best of starts to the 1974 championship. They lost the opening game 9-6 in France, but grew in stature by recording a 9-9 draw in

WILLIEJOHN**MCBRIDE**

Dublin against Wales and then defeating England 26-21 and Scotland 9-6.

While his achievements with Ireland were more a case of what might have been – notably in 1972 when Ireland beat France and England in a championship that wasn't completed because of the Troubles – the opposite applied to his career with the Lions, with whom he won a record 17 Test caps.

The 1962 debut in South Africa was followed by the 1966 trip to New Zealand and Australia. They defeated the Wallabies but were whitewashed 4-0 by the All Blacks, McBride appearing in two of the Tests.

It was much the same story in South Africa two years later, only this time they just avoided a whitewash by drawing one Test. It was little consolation to McBride and his team-mates.

Yet the glory days were just around the corner. Inspired by some of the emerging players that would go on to make Wales the dominant force throughout the decade, the 1971 Lions beat New Zealand in two Tests, losing one and drawing the other to claim the only Lions series victory over New Zealand in history.

It was a triumph that has never been eclipsed, but for McBride the next Lions tour was his finest and the one that will forever be mentioned in the same breath as his name.

Unity was the key to McBride's success as a skipper for the Lions. When asked by Welsh fans to get their Lions shirts signed by the Welsh players, he replied: "There are no Welsh players, no Irish players, no Scottish players, no English players. There are only Lions. If you've 30 of them, one for everybody, you're welcome, we will take them. But there's no division."

The Little Book of **RUGBY** LEGENDS

His attitude to winning or losing was also critical, as he once explained. "It was this old thing of it's not the winning or the losing, it's the taking part that counts. That was a load of bullshit. You went out to South Africa to beat the Springboks in a series."

And beat them they did, winning three of the four Tests and drawing the other. As famous as the victory was his '99' call, which was deployed whenever a team-mate was subjected to violent play and entailed Lions players clobbering their nearest opponent, the message being that the tourists wouldn't be intimidated. Legendary as the call is, McBride plays it down. "It has been overplayed. I would say there were possibly four incidents in all the games and that was about it. It was a good thing because it showed South Africa that the Lions at last were going to stand up and weren't going to take this nonsense. On previous tours they were bullied and we weren't prepared to accept it on this tour."

McBride retired the following year and made his last Ireland appearance in Cardiff, with his side crashing to a 32-4 defeat to Wales. All told he led his country on 12 occasions during his 63-cap career, as well as captaining a World XV against South Africa in 1977.

ABOVE
McBride at the helm of the 1974 Lions.

FAR LEFT
McBride earned his world-renowned reputation in the green of Ireland.

COLIN
MEADS

Name: Colin Earl Meads
Born: 3 June 1936
Country: New Zealand
Position: Lock
Debut: 25 May 1957 v Australia
Caps: 55
Points: 2

When Rugby World, the world's best-selling rugby magazine, was launched in 1960, there was really only one choice as to who to put on the cover: Colin Meads. The man known throughout the rugby world as Pinetree was the archetypal New Zealand rugby player: tough, uncompromising and, above all, a man who had the game in his soul.

Meads, whose brother Stan was also an All Black, played almost all his international rugby at lock but also featured as a flanker and No 8.

A cult figure throughout New Zealand, his home in the aptly named King Country is now a favourite tourist spot, with hundreds of Lions fans who travelled to New Zealand in 2005 taking the time to visit it during their trip.

Legend has it that as part of the training Meads did on his farm, he would run with a sheep under each arm. That adoration is magnified in New Zealand where there is a Colin Meads club, where members wear No 5 jerseys and meet to talk about the great man while reading from his autobiography, Colin Meads: All Black.

His toughness was perhaps best demonstrated in 1970, when he broke his arm playing in South Africa against Eastern Transvaal. Meads emerged from a ruck with a fearful injury but not only did he refuse to leave the field, in one of the hardest places to play rugby in the world, but he finished the match, reportedly saying afterwards: "At least we won the bloody game."

Dubbed 'Pinetree' by his team-mate Kevin Briscoe on the 1958 New Zealand Under-23s tour of Japan, it was an apt nickname and it stuck.

One of the first names on the All Blacks team sheet after his debut in 1957, Meads barely missed a match until his final Test, against the Lions in 1971. That series defeat by the Lions, when Meads was the All Blacks captain, proved a rare low point. His nadir had come in 1967, when he became only the second player to be sent off in a Test match, dismissed by KD Kelleher against Scotland.

Meads was initially played on the flank as the All Blacks possessed fearsome locks in Nev MacEwan and 'Tiny' Hill, but he soon found his way into his more accustomed No 5 shirt.

After representing King Country at primary school and junior level, Meads made his senior representative debut as a 19-year-old against South Auckland Counties in 1955, marking his debut not only with a try but incredibly with a drop-goal too. He was later to score seven Test tries.

COLIN**MEADS**

His Test debut came in 1957 against Australia, but it was in 1960 when he became a legend on the world stage, going on tour to South Africa.

When England toured Australia in the summer of 2006, they played two Test matches, albeit in six days, and then returned to Blighty for an 11-week rest period before the new season. But when the All Blacks went to South Africa in 1960 they played 25 games, the teak-solid Meads featuring in 20 of them.

The All Blacks were imperious in the 1960s and Meads was at the core of their success. From 1965 to 1969, they won a world-record 17 consecutive Tests, as the All Blacks forwards redefined the game.

In Meads's day, of course, there was no World Cup or Super 14 to trophy to hold aloft, so Meads gained his honours from his peers. Although he had his detractors, who claimed his physicality went too far – notably when he ended the career of Australia scrum-half Ken Catchpole in 1968 – he was named Player of the Century at the NZRFU Awards dinner in 1999.

There was no greater honour for Meads than to wear the All Blacks jersey, but in the rest of the world his abilities were recognised when he was invited to play in the South African 75th jubilee (1964), the RFU centenary matches (1971) and captained the President's XV and an Invitation XV against the All Blacks in 1973.

Meads wasn't content with holding an exalted place as a player and went on to be a leading coach and administrator, today still being one of the foremost commentators on New Zealand rugby.

A coach with King Country in the late 1970s, he soon progressed to becoming a national selector, a role he lost when he was part of the outlawed Cavaliers side that went to South Africa in 1986.

After coaching King Country from 1976-81, Meads was a North Island selector 1982-85 before being elected to the national selection panel in

1986. However, he was voted off the panel at the end of that year after being "severely reprimanded" by the NZRFU for coaching the unofficial Cavaliers side.

Chairman of the King Country RFU in 1987, Meads was forgiven for his part in the Cavaliers tour, and elected to the NZRFU council in 1992, later managing the All Blacks in 1994-95.

Stepping down in 1996, he remains closely in touch with the game, recently being part of a panel that reported to the NZRFU on aspects of modern forward play.

LEFT
A man of teak, Meads was one of the greatest All Blacks.

FAR LEFT
Almost every honour the game had to offer arrived at Meads' door.

Outside of rugby, Meads, after initially agreeing to help out for a year, has been involved since his playing days with the Intellectually Handicapped Children's Society, including serving on the national council.

"Meads received just about every honour the game bestowed, including membership of the International Hall of Fame and the New Zealand Sporting Hall of Fame," wrote Lindsay Knight in a profile for the New Zealand Rugby Museum. "There was no dispute when at the end of 1999, New Zealand Rugby Monthly magazine proclaimed him the New Zealand Player of the Century. And in the New Year Honours list of 2001 he was made a New Zealand Companion of Merit, the equivalent of the by then scrapped knighthoods.

"As a sporting legend, Meads is New Zealand's equivalent of Australia's Sir Donald Bradman or the United States of America's Babe Ruth."

CLIFF
MORGAN

Name: Clifford Isaac Morgan
Born: 7 April 1930
Country: Wales
Position: Fly-half
Debut: 10 March 1951 v Ireland
Caps: 29
Points: 9

So often in life a peak follows a trough, and the same certainly applies to Welsh rugby. Following a lean post-war period, Wales finally sprung into action once more and at the centre of it all was Cliff Morgan, a fly-half of exceptional ability who would play a key role in securing not only a Grand Slam but a famous win over the All Blacks.

A talented soccer player, Morgan could potentially have made his name in the round-ball sport – his father rejected the opportunity to play for Tottenham Hotspur – but going to a grammar school soon knocked that idea out of him. Instead, he ended up signing for Cardiff straight from school at the age of 16.

At 20 years of age, he made his debut for Wales against Ireland. Facing him for the Irish was their awesome fly-half Jack Kyle, a player Morgan had marvelled at when he was a teenager. "Two years before I had gone to Penarth with my father to watch Kyle play for the Barbarians," wrote Morgan in his autobiography. " 'Now there's a player you ought to be like', my father had said. He was so beautifully balanced, and had this gift of lulling the opposition into a false sense of security."

While Kyle did teach Morgan a trick or two on his daunting debut, the Welshman came through his baptism of fire with flying colours, helped by the protective care of Rex Willis at scrum-half and Bleddyn Williams and Jack Matthews in the centre. Wales held Ireland to a 3-3 draw.

A losing Test against the Springboks followed in the winter before Morgan had a chance to complete a full Five Nations campaign the next year. Having appeared in the opening three wins of the campaign against England at Twickenham (8-6), Scotland in Cardiff (11-0) and Ireland at Lansdowne Road (14-3), Morgan broke a fibula in a club game against Leicester and was ruled out for the season. It was hard on him, as he had to watch from the stands as Alun Thomas took his place and grabbed a drop-goal to help Wales secure the Grand Slam. "I went to watch and it's funny how selfish you feel in that situation," wrote Morgan. "I wanted Wales to win, yet I didn't want Alun to play too well at outside-half. Then he dropped a goal, which wasn't at all surprising; he was a class act was Alun Thomas."

Morgan returned to the fray for the second game of the Five Nations in 1953 and helped Wales to wins over Scotland, Ireland and France. But as they'd already lost to England, they finished runners-up.

That was more than made up for, however, with the unique double Morgan was part of against the All Blacks. Not only did his Cardiff side manage to turn over the mystical Kiwis 8-3, but he repeated the trick in the colours of Wales as the tourists were beaten 13-8. "I don't think we were a better team than New Zealand," penned Morgan, "but there was a certain spirit in the Welsh side that pulled us through. In those last ten minutes we defended, we fell, we tackled, we caught the ball, scooped it away to touch. All the little things that mattered."

After helping Wales finish joint top of the Five Nations with France in 1954, Morgan headed off on an adventure to Ireland, where he played for Dublin side Bective Rangers – who were promptly renamed Morgan Rangers! "There was lots of nonsense in the Irish papers about Welsh Magicians and Morgan Rangers and so on," said Morgan, who had moved to Ireland to manage a company manufacturing wire ropes. "But whatever I did for Bective was matched by what playing for them did for me."

Playing out of his home country didn't affect his international career as he was selected for the 1955 Lions tour to South Africa – a series that was to live long in the memory. A try in the Lions' 23-22 first-Test victory saw Morgan stamp his mark on the tour, and that was only the beginning. When regular Lions captain Robin Thompson was injured ahead of the third Test in Pretoria, Morgan took over the captaincy, and he inspired his side to a 9-6 victory. "I was glad to have Clem [Thomas] around," said Morgan of that titanic clash. "I was a coward, really. I hated tackling and I didn't like falling on the ball in front of those man-eating South African forwards, but it had to be done in that match. Anyway, Clem looked after us."

The fourth Test may have been lost and the series drawn 2-2, but Cliff Morgan, the miner's son from Rhondda, had left an enormous impression on South African rugby.

Morgan captained Wales to the Five Nations crown the following year and helped them to another couple of top-two finishes before hanging up his boots in 1958. He had been lined up to captain the 1959 Lions tour to New Zealand but felt he could no longer afford to take the time off work.

His headline-grabbing days weren't over, however, as Morgan embarked on a successful career with the BBC, eventually becoming head of outside broadcasts despite suffering a stroke when he was 41. It was Morgan who provided the now immortal commentary to the most famous try of all time – the one scored by Gareth Edwards against the All Blacks in 1973.

Even from behind the mike, Morgan was a legend: "Kirkpatrick to Williams. This is great stuff. Phil Bennett covering, chased by Alistair Scown. Brilliant, oh, that's brilliant. John Williams… Pullin, John Dawes. Great dummy. David, Tom David, the halfway line. Brilliant by Quinnell. This is Gareth Edwards. A dramatic start. What a score!"

LEFT
Morgan made his name in the famous Cardiff shirt.

FAR LEFT
A Lion in 1955, he became a legend in South Africa.

FRANCOIS
PIENAAR

Name: Jacobus Francois Pienaar
Born: 2 January 1967
Country: South Africa
Position: Flanker
Debut: 26 June 1993 v France
Caps: 29
Points: 15

It could be argued that every World Cup final is special to those involved, and every image of a captain lifting that famous trophy is poignant in its way – whether it be David Kirk in 1987, Nick Farr-Jones in 1991, John Eales in 1999 or Martin Johnson in 2003. But there is one final that stands head and shoulders above the rest: the 1995 World Cup in South Africa. The moment Springboks skipper Francois Pienaar accepted the Webb Ellis Cup from South African president Nelson Mandela will live long in the memory of not only their countrymen but also everyone who was able to witness it, either in person or as one of the millions tuned into the final.

Sadly for such a great team, the fact that New Zealand were even there was insignificant.

Timing is, of course, everything and the story of how Pienaar's men won the World Cup for South Africa – at the first time of asking, after the country had been excluded from the events in 1987 and 1991 – symbolised the change taking place in the Rainbow Nation. That it was Pienaar, a blond, white Afrikaner, who collected the trophy from Mandela, the black leader who had brought about such fundamental change in South Africa, made the moment all the more unique. And the fact Mandela wore a replica of Pienaar's No 6 shirt summed up the new spirit of unity that prevailed in the Republic at that time. "It's been the best six weeks of my life," said Pienaar in the moments after the match. "We did not have 63,000 fans behind us today, we had 43 million South Africans.

Reflecting later on the momentous presentation at Ellis Park, Pienaar said: "When he gave us the trophy he said: 'Thank you for what you have done for South Africa'. I said we could never do what he had done for South Africa. I almost felt like hugging him but it wasn't appropriate, I guess."

As a player Pienaar, a hard-hitting blindside flanker, was clearly talented, but it was his leadership skills that stood him apart. From his very first cap against France in 1993, he was made captain (replacing the legendary Naas Botha) and he never relinquished the armband until the last of his 29 appearances in 1996, a 29-18 defeat against New Zealand.

His ability to lead was certainly put to the test. During the 1995 World Cup, South Africa's semi-final against France was in danger of being called off due to heavy rain. Had that decision been taken, France would have proceeded to the final because of South Africa's poor disciplinary record earlier in the competition. While the side waited to hear their fate, Pienaar's charisma and leadership came to the fore.

"Francois Pienaar, in the two hours before that World Cup semifinal, was brilliant," wrote Springbok wing Chester Williams in his autobiography. "He showed calmness, composure and enthusiasm. He kept focusing on the occasion and he kept channelling all the energy towards the match. At no stage did he look rattled. He communicated what was going on as if it were all part of the master plan.

"I don't believe Pienaar should have captained South Africa at the World Cup. I don't think he deserved to be there as a player… but I will never detract from Pienaar's contribution to our victory in the changing room that Saturday. It was pivotal to our attitude when we eventually got on to the field. It was crucial to us being crowned world champions a week later when we beat the All Blacks in the final."

Hailing from a working-class Afrikaner family, Pienaar became a student of law at Rand Afrikaans University, gaining his place through an athletic scholarship. But on the field he didn't have the quickest rise to the top. He made his debut for the Springboks at the relatively late age of 26 having made his provincial debut for Transvaal (now the Golden Lions) four years previously.

In 1994, he captained Transvaal to Currie Cup success and such was his contribution to province and country that Rugby World awarded him the accolade of International Player of the Year.

His greatest moment came a year later with the World Cup triumph, something he recalls vividly. "I fell right to my knees," said Pienaar about the moment the cup was South Africa's. "I'm a Christian and I wanted to say a quick prayer for being in such a wonderful event, not because of the winning.

"Then all of a sudden I realised the whole team was around me, which was a special moment. Lifting the trophy was unbelievable. I can't describe the feeling as I wouldn't do it justice."

He wasn't to know it, but Pienaar's international career had little more than a year left to run. After eight more caps, which included a European tour and competing in the first-ever Tri-Nations, he was sensationally dropped by Andre Markgraaff in 1996. The coach accused him of feigning injury and a disgusted Pienaar never pulled on the green and gold jersey again.

Instead, he left South Africa for England to start a mini revolution at English club Saracens, initially as player-coach. With the floodgates having been opened due to the advent of professionalism, he was given an open chequebook to bring some of rugby's biggest names to the club. Unfortunately for him, Rob Andrew was given the same opportunity at Newcastle and subsequently beat him to the title. Saracens did, however, win the 1998 Tetley's Bitter Cup and qualified for the Heineken Cup. They've never looked like repeating Pienaar's early success since.

In 2000, Pienaar hung up his boots and added the role of chief executive to his coaching brief, but the failure to bring more silverware to the club cost him both jobs and he stepped down in 2002.

ABOVE
Pienaar's greatest moment, receiving the World Cup trophy from President Nelson Mandela, in 1995.

MIDDLE
Pienaar ended his career, in English rugby, with Saracens.

FAR LEFT
Pienaar brought silverware to Saracens, with their Tetley Bitter Cup final win, in 1998.

FRIK
DUPREEZ

Name: Frederick Christoffel Hendrik du Preez
Born: 28 November 1935
Country: South Africa
Position: Lock
Debut: 7 January 1961 v England
Caps: 38
Points: 11

When Frik du Preez was declared South African rugby's Player of the 20th Century, there wasn't much dissent in one of the most passionate rugby countries in the world, such was his standing in the game. In many ways the award was remarkable as he survived challenges from modern-day players like Francois Pienaar and Joost van der Westhulzen, having played his final game for South Africa in 1971. It shows how untouchable he was.

Du Preez was an uncompromising second-row forward from Rustenberg, who ruled the roost in the unforgiving world of the pack for a decade.

He made his debut at Twickenham in 1961, immediately revealing his abilities to a European audience at a time when some of the greats from the southern hemisphere went unheralded in the north.

It comes as no surprise to discover that du Preez kicked off with a win in that clash against England (5-0) and from then until his final match in 1971, an 18-6 victory against Australia, he only suffered eight defeats in Springbok colours.

He made his debut as a second-row but also played on the flank in an international career that lasted 11 seasons. The abilities he picked up in the back row would serve him well throughout his career, and one of his most memorable moments came, as commentator Bill McLaren was often heard to say, "on the hoof".

That magic moment arrived in the 1968 series against the British & Irish Lions when, following a lineout, du Preez scored a storming try, running in from 40 metres with a lung-bursting, unstoppable dash. Tom Kiernan stood in front of him but, as the South African writer AC Parker vividly concluded, the Lions full-back might as well have tried to stop a locomotive going at full speed.

That try was typical of the all-round footballing skills demonstrated by du Preez. Of the more modern era, think John Eales and you are getting close to what du Preez was like. Both men were accomplished locks but also had skills rarely associated with those in the engine room. Each had superb handling ability, could get around the pitch swiftly and, most unusually, could kick goals, du Preez landing two penalties and a conversion in his Test-match career.

Those 1968 Springboks, with du Preez at their heart, inflicted a 3-0 series win on the Lions and a 2-0 victory in France. A year later, Australia were put to the sword in a 4-0 whitewash.

FRIK DU **PREEZ**

Those who saw him in his pomp believe that du Preez, renowned as a man of great humility, would have suited modern-day rugby and would have thrived in a sport where ball-handling skills have become more paramount as the decades have passed.

He prospered in an era when lifting in the lineout wasn't allowed and his ability to leap from a standing start was legendary. Springbok team-mate Tiny Naude said: "Frik wasn't a very big man but he was very athletic. He could jump up to a man's waist, whereas when I jumped my feet hardly left the ground!"

The great Colin Meads remembers du Preez as an opponent who "could jump up and clap his hands above the crossbar," adding: "I struggled to touch the bloody thing."

Commentator McLaren was another one to recognise du Preez's pre-eminence in the lineout. "He was one of the greatest lineout technicians, with a standing jump measurement that was mind-boggling considering that he was only 6ft 2in and 15 and a half stone," said McLaren.

"Du Preez developed from a fly-half at school to become one of the most gifted locks of all time. He was a dependable lineout purveyor, with educated hands and a powerful boot, and a grinding scrummager who was astonishingly quick for his size. In his first ten Internationals he never lost. He once sent over a 75-yard dropped goal in Pretoria and he had the honour of leading the Springboks onto the field for his final Test, against Australia in 1971."

This man of many talents was rewarded for his endeavours when he was named as a founder member of the International Rugby Hall of

Fame in 1997, only one of two Springboks (with Danie Craven) in that list of initial inductees.

Craven, for many years the man in charge of South African rugby, paid this tribute to du Preez: "South African rugby is an inspiration for everyone in our country who is interested in the game, and a source of wonder for those people beyond our borders. One of the most important factors responsible for this is the fact that throughout the history of Springbok rugby there have been great players and great personalities.

"Amongst these greats is Frik du Preez. As long as rugby is played in our country, people who know Frik or knew him, or people who heard of him or read about him, will have a connection with him, and that will enrich our rugby just as Frik did on the playing fields."

Du Preez's influence on the Springboks continued into the professional era, and along with Francois Pienaar he was chosen to hand out the shirts to the South Africa team during the 2005 Tri-Nations Championship.

When du Preez, who also played for Northern Transvaal, retired in 1971, he had won a record 38 caps for South Africa. Including his non-Test appearances, he played 87 times for South Africa, scoring an even 87 points.

LEFT
Frik du Preez tackles an opponent in a match against Southern Counties in 1960.

FAR LEFT
Du Preez (top right) beats France's Elie Cester (top, left) to the line out ball during a Rest of the World training session, 1971.

PHILIPPE
SELLA

Name: Philippe Jean-Paul Sella
Born: 14 February 1962
Country: France
Position: Centre
Debut: 31 October 1982 v Romania
Caps: 111
Points: 125

One of the key exponents of France's champagne rugby, Philippe Sella's skill and magic is surpassed only by his incredible longevity. The centre stayed at the top of rugby's tree for 111 caps over 13 years, dazzling spectators and befuddling opponents. Sella wasn't shy of the rough stuff either, as former France coach Jacques Fouroux explained when he described him as having "the strength of a bull but the touch of a piano player". Following the 2006 Six Nations, Sella lay third in the all-time list for most capped players, four ahead of current France captain Fabien Pelous.

Jonathan Davies, in selecting Sella in his all-time Five Nations XV, was full of praise for the Frenchman. "Inside-centre is a spot where there is no competition. Philippe Sella was big, strong and quick. He scored tries and was defensively very sound. He played in a very good French side and one of the main reasons for that was because they had 'the Prince' at inside-centre."

Even though his international career started on the low that was defeat to Romania in 1982, Sella still stood out as a talent to watch, despite ending up in hospital for the night with concussion. An Agen player throughout his career until Saracens came calling, his ability to be both brutal and beautiful was admired by many, not least Jamie Salmon, who played in the centre for both New Zealand and England. "As an All Black I'd played against the excellent Roland Bertranne, but Sella was one of the first players to have a major physical presence in midfield."

Following the disappointment of defeat to Romania, Sella helped France to two victories over Argentina, scoring the first two of his 30 Test tries for France.

He was back on the scoresheet on his Five Nations debut at Twickenham, Les Bleus beating England 19-15 on their way to a tied championship with Ireland.

In the 1984 championship, Sella helped France win in Cardiff for the first time since

1968. While adding the scalps of Ireland and England, Scotland proved an insurmountable stumbling block and toppled the French 21-12 at Murrayfield. The win gave Scotland the Grand Slam and left France licking their wounds in second place.

A similar fate would befall them in 1985. This time France remained unbeaten, but draws with Ireland and England left them trailing the Irish in top spot.

The following year saw Sella take his game to new heights. He became one of the select few to score in every Five Nations match of a championship, with several memorable tries helping France to a shared title with the Scots. Against Ireland the ball went through 21 pairs of hands before Sella crossed the whitewash, against Wales he hauled several defenders with him as he touched down and against the English another flowing French move from their own half was brought to a successful conclusion by the Prince. The latter try prompted Nigel Starmer-Smith to proclaim that there was "no better tribute for the outstanding player in the championship".

The summer that followed included a drawn series with Argentina, and defeats by Australia and New Zealand. Later that year France took revenge against the All Blacks as the Kiwis fell 16-3 in Nantes. Admittedly, the New Zealanders had won the first Test 19-7 (with Sella scoring), but it was a huge win for the French nonetheless, with the inaugural World Cup looming at the end of the season.

Sella's brilliance of 1986 proved a foundation stone for unqualified success in the 1987 Five Nations as France claimed their first outright title since 1981 – and once again it was with a Grand Slam. The 19-15 away win over England featured one of Sella's finest moments, an interception score from deep inside his own half. "We were under big pressure from the English at the time and the game was still not won," recalled Sella. "I can't explain why exactly – maybe it's the French flair – but I intercepted the ball and 70 metres later had scored a try."

France were among the favourites for the World Cup that summer and they proved their standing with an epic 30-24 semi-final win over Australia in Sydney. Unfortunately, the European champions had little left to give and they were humbled 29-9 by New Zealand in a one-sided final.

Coping with World Cup disappointment in the only way they knew how, Sella's France took a share in the next Five Nations with Wales before winning the title outright in 1989. It was Sella's penultimate Five Nations title as they achieved it only once more – in 1993 – during his career.

The 1987 World Cup final was also to be Sella's grandest stage as England put paid to French hopes in the 1991 quarter-finals and the weather combined with an inspired South Africa to end their interest at the semi-final stage in 1995. Sella bowed out of international rugby in the third-place play-off victory over England, before enjoying a successful spell at Saracens in his twilight years, the highlight being a sparkling cup final rout of Wasps in 1998. Sella played his last competitive game at 36.

Asked which of his caps he remembers most, Sella points to his 94th cap, against Australia at the Parc des Princes in 1993. "That was the day I broke Serge Blanco's record for international caps. Serge had rung me that morning to tell me he couldn't make it to the ceremony. When it came to distributing the jerseys, Pierre Berbizier, the coach, gave one to everyone except me. Then the changing-room door opened and in came Serge with my jersey in his hand. I have to admit I was fighting back the tears. That was one of the proudest moments of my career."

WAISALE
SEREVI

Name: Waisale Tikoisolomoni Serevi
Born: 20 May 1968
Country: Fiji
Position: Utility back
Debut: 7 October 1989 v Belgium
Caps: 40
Points: 221

It's ironic that one of the greatest talents world rugby has seen never really made his mark in the 15-a-side game. Rarely has there been a player who can produce so much magic with the oval ball as Waisale Tikoisolomoni Serevi. With the skills to make the ball do things that mere mortals can only dream of doing, Suva-born Serevi has delighted fans the world over with his dazzling array of tricks, flicks and kicks. His vision is unparalleled; one minute he appears to be going nowhere but into a dead end, the next he's conjured some space and sent a team-mate scuttling in for another Serevi-inspired score.

But impressive as his skill set is, it's in the vast expanse of the sevens game that we have got to appreciate it most. While his sevens career has involved more gongs than a trophy-maker's workshop, his 15-a-side résumé is less striking.

It began in 1989 in Liege when Fiji took on the rugby minnow that is Belgium and ran amok, racking up 76 points with none in return. Serevi grabbed two scores in the far-from-glamorous fixture.

From such low-key beginnings, Serevi managed to win 40 caps for his country up until his international retirement at the 2003 World Cup. Scoring 221 Test points, he certainly made a contribution, especially when you consider that of the 40 caps, 16 were from the bench. And he achieved the feat of appearing at three World Cups, so even though his exploits in Test rugby aren't regarded as much to write home about, he still achieved far more than most.

On a club level, things were similarly stop-start. His talent was recognised by Australia's World Cup-winning coach Bob Dwyer, who snapped him for English club Leicester Tigers. But the presence of South African duo Joel Stransky at fly-half and Michael Horak at full-back forced Serevi onto the wing. Here, he was able to produce moments of brilliance, but his defensive frailties were also exposed as he managed to delight and disappoint the

Welford Road faithful in equal measure. Failing to settle into the English game, he moved on to France and lower-level rugby at Stade Bordelais.

To talk about the negatives, however, is to downplay the contribution Serevi has made to the global game. He may have struggled with the 15-a-side format but in sevens he came alive. So much so that Serevi and the abridged game are synonymous with one another. Ask any rugby fan to name a sevens player and the answer will probably be Serevi, surely the greatest exponent of the sport there has been. And there are plenty of people to back that assertion up. Paul Treu, the South Africa sevens coach, said of the Fijian: "I played against Serevi and he was the master of the game; if people talked about sevens, they talked about Serevi."

Serevi's list of honours in the game speaks volumes: two World Cups (both as captain), five Hong Kong Sevens titles, two Commonwealth Games silver medals and a gold from the World Games is just the tip of the iceberg.

As if to consolidate his legendary status, Serevi completed a fairy-tale comeback at the 2005 Sevens World Cup in Hong Kong. In international exile and playing club rugby in the lower reaches of the English league with Staines, Fiji coach Wayne Pivac recalled the maestro for the World Cup. "He's a wee man who we call 'Wai'," said Pivac at the time. "He's world famous when it comes to sevens, he's a great guy, a good leader and obviously has been a fantastic player. He hasn't quite got the legs he had when he was 26. He's 36 now, but still he's got the vision and the class and knows the game inside out. He was one of the first people I wanted to get involved."

LEFT
Here on his way to helping Fiji lift the World Sevens crown in 2005.

FAR LEFT
Serevi also won 40 caps for his country at 15-a-side.

Pivac's decision to recall Serevi paid dividends as Fiji bucked the sevens trend that has seen the New Zealanders dominate the game in recent years. Not only did Fiji win but it was with a style and panache orchestrated by the master himself. In the semi-final, Serevi scored in sudden-death extra time to beat England 24-19. He then pulled the strings as Fiji toppled the Kiwis 29-19 in the final, reminding the world just why Serevi is so adored in his homeland. He was named Player of the Tournament and the feat of becoming world champions ensured that a public holiday was declared in Fiji.

Though his 38th birthday was to come and go before the end of the 2006 IRB Sevens series, Serevi was still going strong as player-coach of the Fiji side. And after their triumph in the Singapore Sevens in April, Fiji led the series by 10 points with just two events to go. New Zealand, perennial champions, were out of contention.

What, then, is the secret to Serevi's success? "I enjoy playing rugby, this is my life," he said. "I look after myself, I don't drink and I don't smoke, so that's why I'm still enjoying playing rugby.

"They asked me when would I stop playing rugby, but while you still enjoy it day to day you might as well keep on doing it.

"One day I will stop. I didn't want to regret stopping this year and saying that I could have done one more year. I thank God for giving me the power and strength to keep playing and enjoying what I love best: playing rugby sevens."

The Fijians thank God for Serevi too.

JONNY
WILKINSON

Name: Jonathan Peter Wilkinson
Born: 25 May 1979
Country: England
Position: Fly-half
Debut: 4 April 1998 v Ireland
Caps: 55
Points: 849

When Jonny Wilkinson kicked the winning drop-goal in the 2003 World Cup final, he had the sporting world at his feet. He was the world's most famous rugby player, the best outside-half and had just delivered the Webb Ellis Cup to Twickenham for the first time in history.

From then on things started to go wrong, with a list of injuries that would have finished most players. Shoulder, bicep, knee and groin injuries mounted one upon another, ensuring that, by the end of the 2006 Six Nations, he hadn't pulled on an England shirt since that famous day in Sydney nearly two-and-a-half years earlier.

Although Wilkinson was just 24 when that right-footed drop-goal bisected the uprights in Sydney's Olympic Stadium, he had already done enough to earn legendary status.

The boy from Surrey made his international debut at the age of 18, coming on as a substitute in the closing moments of England's 35-17 Five Nations win at home to Ireland in 1998 and becoming his country's youngest full international for 71 years.

And although his first start in the England No 10 shirt came in an infamous 76-0 defeat in Australia, the experience only intensified his determination to make it to the top.

After having a cameo role in the 1999 World Cup, he started to set the rugby world alight, beginning with a championship record of 78 points in the 2000 Six Nations, when he was just 20. That June he missed England's first-Test defeat by South Africa with food poisoning. Yet a week later he climbed off his sick bed to kick all 27 points as England won 27-22 in Bloemfontein, a performance described by coach Clive Woodward as "awesome".

By 2001, Wilkinson had become England's leading point-scorer of all time, surpassing his club coach Rob Andrew at Newcastle. The following year, he enhanced his reputation as one of the world's best players with a starring role in a trio of England wins over South Africa, New Zealand and Australia.

And once World Cup year cranked into gear he was unstoppable, inspiring England to a Grand Slam, with 77 points in the Six Nations, and summer wins over New Zealand and Australia, that set them up for victory in Sydney.

Even before the final against Australia, Wilkinson left an indelible mark, scoring all of England's 24 points in the semi-final win over France. He finished the final with 15 points and ended the tournament as top point-scorer with 113.

Wilkinson came under huge pressure during that World Cup in Australia. He became the biggest sports star in the country and saw his every move under scrutiny. The rest of the England team were in awe over the way his mental strength kept him on top and, once the Webb Ellis Cup was won, Martin Johnson had some special words of praise for Wilkinson.

"I can't say enough about Wilko," said England's skipper. "There is a lot of pressure on him and he gets built up to a degree where people expect superhuman stuff from him, and most of the stuff he does is verging on that.

To call him a kicker doesn't do him justice because the work he puts in on the field and in all aspects of his game is fantastic. He is a very special player, a very special person."

After Sydney, Wilkinson became one of the most recognisable faces in the sporting world and he even had the chance to play American Football. But when the offer came along the reaction of Woodward summed up Wilkinson's value to rugby.

"I wanted to create superstar players in rugby like Jonny and we've done that," Woodward said. "But we have to make sure we pay them. We could lose Jonny to American Football, for example, and we just can't do that. I wouldn't let that happen. People play sport because of people like Tiger Woods and David Beckham and Jonny Wilkinson."

An obsessive trainer in his early 20s, Wilkinson has admitted his routine played its part in his catalogue of injuries. Wilkinson said: "The reason this is happening is the shearing of the joints from the repetitive nature of the kicking. I understand that – I've put a lot of strain on myself. The two-hour kicking sessions will always be with me. If I have a problem with the kicking, I almost feel I have no choice, it's second nature to carry on until I've got it right.

But for years I've been compounding two-hour session upon two-hour session. I'm going to have to be a bit cuter now. I know I cannot afford to think like that every single day."

Andy Robinson's first act when becoming England coach in October 2004 was to appoint Wilkinson as England captain, taking over from Lawrence Dallaglio. But injury ensured he was never given the chance to wear the captain's armband for a second time, having led England against Italy in the 2003 Six Nations. "He is a natural leader," said Robinson, "and he consistently demonstrates the energy and commitment I feel is essential to be captain of England. Jonny is in every way the right player to take on this challenge."

In 2002 he was awarded an MBE, becoming the youngest rugby union player to receive a New Year honour, in succession to Gareth Edwards, who was 27. An OBE followed for Wilkinson after the World Cup.

Despite his injury problems, he was fit enough to go on the 2005 Lions tour, where he won two caps to add to the three he won in a losing series in Australia in 2001. Selected in an unfamiliar role of centre against the All Blacks, he played the first Test but was taken off injured in the second. He was the only choice as 2003 BBC Sports Personality of the Year.

As England's 2006 summer tour approaches, Wilkinson has scored 817 points in 52 Tests for England, putting him sixth on the all-time list.

JPR**WILLIAMS**

Name: John Peter Rhys Williams
Born: 2 March 1949
Country: Wales
Position: Full-back
Debut: 1 February 1969 v Scotland
Caps: 55
Points: 36

You know you've made it in the sporting world when people refer to you just by your first name or initials. Mention 'JPR' and everyone from Bridgend to Ballymena, from Cardiff to Christchurch, knows who you're taking about: John Peter Rhys Williams. JPR – so named to differentiate him from another John Williams in the Wales team, winger JJ – became a legend in the 1970s as a pivotal part of the Wales side that swept all before them in Europe. He was also one of the few men to play in all eight Lions Tests during the victorious tours of 1971 and 1974. An orthopaedic surgeon, JPR turned down the chance to make it three Lions tours in 1977 to focus on forthcoming medical exams.

Born in Cardiff, JPR played his club rugby for Bridgend and London Welsh, during a glittering career that brought 55 Wales caps, his list of honours including three Grand Slams and six Triple Crowns. In 45 Five Nations matches, he finished on the losing side just seven times, and not once against England.

Not a prolific try-scorer, JPR was so often the architect of tries for Wales and the Lions. His most memorable intervention came at Eden Park in 1971, when he landed a 50-yard drop-goal in the fourth Test that put the Lions into a 14-11 lead. The game ended 14-14 and the Lions had won the series 2-1.

And yet JPR could have been lost to another sport as he was an accomplished tennis player, making a huge impact at international level. JPR played tennis for Great Britain, and lifted the 1966 Junior Wimbledon. He also won a Welsh junior tennis title and played in the first professional tennis tournament, the British Open at Bournemouth, in 1968. However, all of Wales breathed a sigh of relief when JPR put down his racquet and picked up a rugby ball full time.

John Dawes, his team-mate in 1971, was unequivocal about JPR's influence both Wales and the Lions . "He was simply the best full-back of his type," said the former Lions captain. "He was a fearless tackler, had tremendous courage and was supremely confident. He couldn't spell the word loser. When he'd stay at my place and play cards with my kids, he'd never let them win, telling them, 'Let that be a lesson in life; you've got to win'."

Gareth Edwards is another to appreciate JPR's competitive instinct. In 1975, with Wales coasting towards a huge win over Ireland at Cardiff, Edwards threw out a loose pass that brought a consolation try for Willie Duggan. JPR gave Edwards a rollicking that went along the lines of: "How dare you let them cross my line!"

On another occasion, he retired from a match having had his face stamped on, only to stitch up the injury and return to the field!

JPR was first capped by Wales in 1969, as a 19-year-old, before embarking on his record-breaking career. He was to prove the scourge of England, beating them on no fewer than 14 occasions, three in junior rugby and 11 in Test matches, scoring five tries in the process. In fact, during his 12-year international career he only missed two games against England (in 1974 and 1980) and Wales lost them both.

His career had countless highlights but high on the list are his three Grand Slams, in 1971, 1976 and 1978, the latter secured after JPR made a crucial shoulder-barge tackle on Jean-Francois Gourdon near the corner flag. "Playing for Wales at Cardiff Arms Park in the Seventies was a hell of an experience," JPR said. "I suppose it must have been like being on a drug."

JPR was an initial inductee into the International Rugby Hall of Fame, in 1997.

"Perhaps it was just the way he played," explained former Wales captain Eddie Butler in The Observer. "He was so competitive and committed that he used to shut down all the instincts that have been triggers of fear ever since man found that unarmed combat with a sabre-toothed tiger was inadvisable.

"JPR was not big but he played huge. He had an unerring eye for the high ball and could sidestep as well as bounce juggernauts. He had a deft touch too and no moment was sweeter than when he dropped the goal from way back in the fourth Test against the All Blacks in 1971. The match was drawn; the Lions won the series 2-1, the only time they've ever beaten New Zealand."

Rock-solid in defence, it was through his skills as a counter-attacking full-back that JPR earned his worldwide reputation.

After Wales won the 1978 Grand Slam, JPR captained Wales five times, taking them through the 1979 Five Nations Triple Crown. He announced his retirement from international rugby, but later reversed his decision, playing against New Zealand in the autumn of 1980 and then England and Scotland in the 1981 Five Nations. He was dropped after the defeat at Murrayfield, a sad way to bow out, but his rugby-playing days were to last much, much longer.

His tremendous fitness levels meant that even at 48 he was still turning out for Tondu 3rds, unable to give up the game he loves. "Some people say I'm mad but I'm loving every minute of it. I'll have to retire when I'm 50, but I will continue to play competitive squash," said JPR at the time.

"They wouldn't pick me at openside flanker until the cup match – they said I'm too slow – so normally I pack down at No 8 or blindside.

"At junior level the rugby is like the game I used to play. The refreshing thing is that the players aren't too full of themselves, unlike some at senior level."

A product of Millfield School, along with Edwards, JPR graduated to veterans' rugby, making several appearances at the Bermuda Classic. We weren't going to get rid of him that easily and thank goodness for that!

LEFT
The great man had an astonishing 19-year career for Wales.

FAR LEFT
JPR was honoured by the Queen in 1977, being made an MBE.

KEITH
WOOD

Name: Keith Gerard Mallinson Wood
Born: 27 January 1972
Country: Ireland
Position: Hooker
Debut: 5 June 1994 v Australia
Caps: 58
Points: 75

Injuries played far too big a role in the career of the 'flying potato' that was Keith Wood, and he should have won more than the 58 caps he managed from 1994 to 2003. The son of an Ireland international (Gordon Wood won 29 caps at prop), Wood's playing days began with Garryowen, where he won titles in 1992 and 1994 before accepting an offer to join English club Harlequins.

Enjoying some success at club level with the London side, Wood had a tough start to life with Ireland. He sat on the bench during the 1994 Five Nations and had to watch as, first up, his team-mates were hammered 35-15 by France. His Ireland debut followed on the summer tour to Australia, where his passion and all-action style in a losing cause won him the admiration of the Aussie public.

The next season he made his Five Nations debut in the 20-8 defeat by England at Lansdowne Road. Wood's early record for Ireland in the Five Nations read: played 11, won one, lost 10. He experienced life at the bottom as Ireland collected the wooden spoon three seasons in succession from 1996. The following year they dragged themselves up to fourth. In the book Five Go To War, Wood admitted that despite the lack of initial success, he never fell out of love with the competition: "In terms of success, the tournament has been less than favourable to me. My first win came against Wales at Wembley in 1999. I played my first Five Nations match in 1995. Yet after all those years of disappointment I love it all the more. It must be the masochist in me. Months after breaking my duck, I can still feel the glow of success emanating from that one win. Just one win! God only knows how I would react if we were to win the championship."

Luckily for Wood, while he waited for success in the Five Nations, he had the small matter of the 1997 Lions tour to South Africa to take his mind off things. Starting in the crucial first two Tests (he missed only the third match, a dead rubber as the Lions had tied up the series), Wood was an influential figure not just for his work rate on the pitch but for the way he encouraged the camaraderie off it. Donald McRae was one of many to be impressed by Wood, as he wrote in Winter Colours. "Keith Wood personified what was best about the Lions. He was outrageously passionate and committed. But he also listened as well as he talked. And whether the Lions were in Vanderbylpark or in Durban, I had my most stimulating conversations with him. He was as ready to entertain me with stories about rugby fervour in Limerick as he was keen to hear about the wild streets of Johannesburg. He would tell me about some of his witty encounters with South African girls and then a thing or two about the ancient art of falconry. That was Keith Wood, a bald but brilliant 25-year-old – an all-round sort of guy. But, above all else, he was a son of Limerick."

Eager as Wood was to help the Lions bond as a unit, however, he was quick to point out that it would be a different story when they all returned home. "I've told these new pals of mine that when we next play against each other, I'm going to kick them in the nuts if I get the chance!" he said. "I expect them to do the same to me and have a pint with me afterwards."

As a player, Wood led from the front, charging around the field and scoring an obscene number of tries for a front-row forward – he managed 15 for Ireland, including four in a 1999 World Cup match against the USA.

In 2000, despite an opening-day hammering by England (50-18), Wood led his side to third spot in the first Six Nations thanks to three victories, the most notable of which was an epic 27-25 win over the French – Ireland's first win in Paris for 28 years.

That same year, Wood had returned to Ireland to play one season with Munster in an attempt to inspire them to a Heineken Cup victory. He almost succeeded, too, as Munster were beaten 9-8 in the final by Northampton. He returned to Harlequins the next season.

Life got even better for Ireland in the 2001 Six Nations. Although Wood was missing for three of the matches, he featured in the 41-22 win over Italy and the 22-15 defeat of France. In a tournament disrupted by a foot-and-mouth crisis, England went to Dublin in the autumn in search of their first Grand Slam of the professional era. Despite being hot favourites, they never recovered from a

17th-minute try by Wood, who thundered over from a lineout move, and Ireland were left to celebrate a 20-14 success. The Irish lost out for the title to England on points difference. It was the closest Wood ever got to the Six Nations crown.

A Lions tour was also on the agenda for 2001 and again Wood was an automatic selection for the trip to Australia. He played in all three Tests but, unlike in South Africa, this time the series was lost 2-1.

As a final stop on Wood's roller-coaster Test exploits, he led Ireland to the World Cup in Australia. Facing Fabian Galthie's France in the quarter-final, the losing captain faced a disappointing end to their international career. Sadly for Wood, Galthie would carry on to play another match as Ireland crashed 43-21 and the Test arena bade farewell to one of its biggest characters.

"My desire's still there. I'd like to play for another 10 years if I had the chance," said Wood at the time. "The heart is willing, the head is willing, but the body's had enough."

ABOVE
Wood scored an incredible number of tries for a hooker, grabbing 75 points in his 58 Tests.

FAR LEFT
Wood moved to Harlequins, here helping them win the European Shield in 2001.

The Little Book of
CRICKET
LEGENDS
RALPH**DELLOR** and STEPHEN**LAMB**

The Little Book of
FOOTBALL
LEGENDS
GRAHAM**BETTS**

The Little Book of
GRAND PRIX
LEGENDS
PHILIP**RABY**

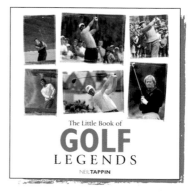

The Little Book of
GOLF
LEGENDS
NEIL**TAPPIN**

THE PICTURES IN THIS BOOK WERE PROVIDED COURTESY OF THE FOLLOWING:

GETTY**IMAGES**
101 Bayham Street, London NW1 0AG

EMPICS
www.empics.com

Concept, Original Design and Art Direction:
VANESSA **and** KEVIN**GARDNER**

Design and Artwork by: JANE**STEPHENS**

Image research: ELLIE**CHARLESTON**

PUBLISHED BY GREEN UMBRELLA PUBLISHING

Publishers:
JULES**GAMMOND and** VANESSA**GARDNER**

Series Editor: VANESSA**GARDNER**

Written by: PAUL**MORGAN and** ALEX**MEAD**